every day is a good day

In this book by Indigenous Women, let us now acquaint ourselves and learn from those who have withstood the insatiable rages of the weak, who have used rifles, bad laws, atomic bombs, chemical and biological warfare to make their disastrous impression on the world. Let us who have suffered so much, and those who have been ignorant of suffering, grow our hearts again to their utter fullness. Hearing these voices, let us know the tide is beginning to turn, that knowledge of the way of balance has not been lost. Let us welcome home in ourselves, and in the world, the wisdom of the strong.
—Alice Walker, author, *The Color Purple*

For the millennia, the women's centrality in the role of Native communities is undisputed. Here, Wilma Mankiller has invoked the articulate and compelling voices of contemporary Native women to address issues so critical to the continuance of the Native cultural experience.
—Richard West, director,
National Museum of the American Indian

Reading Every Day Is a Good Day *is like sitting down with a wise group of women friends who are generous enough to share life's lessons with you. Since these Native American women have layers of wisdom that younger cultures have yet to discover, joining their circle could balance and even save your life.*
—Marlo Thomas, actor and activist

---

every day is a good day

Reflections by Contemporary Indigenous Women

Memorial Edition

Wilma Mankiller

Forewords by Louise Erdrich and
Vine Deloria Jr.

Introduction by Gloria Steinem

Fulcrum Publishing
Golden, Colorado

Library of Congress Cataloging-in-Publication Data

Mankiller, Wilma Pearl, 1945-2010.
    Every day is a good day : reflections by contemporary indigenous women
/ Wilma Mankiller ; forewords by Louise Erdrich and Vine Deloria, Jr. ;
introduction by Gloria Steinem. -- Memorial ed.
        p. cm.
    Includes bibliographical references.
    ISBN 978-1-55591-691-6 (pbk.)
    1. Indian women--Psychology. 2. Indian women--Social conditions. 3.
Indian women--Biography. 4. Indian philosophy. I. Title.
    E98.W8M25 2011
    970.004'97--dc22

                                        2011004322

Printed in the United States of America
0 9 8 7 6 5 4 3 2 1

Interior design: Ann W. Douden

Fulcrum Publishing
4690 Table Mountain Drive, Suite 100
Golden, Colorado 80403
(800) 992-2908 • (303) 277-1623
www.fulcrumbooks.com

The main difference between our people
and the world around us is
our thankfulness and respect for the Earth,
our environment, and the natural world.
In our way, every day is a good day.
—Audrey Shenandoah, Onondaga

We Native Americans are varied hues in
a bronzed and battered Native world and
present an uneven view of tribal traditions.
—Dr. Beatrice Medicine, Lakota

---

contents

foreword

Louise Erdrich

When this book was first published, Wilma Mankiller came to the bookstore I own in Minneapolis, Birchbark Books. That she would agree to come to the store in spite of her precarious health and her many responsibilities both surprised and moved me. It was clear to me that she deeply cared about this book. She was committed to giving Native women a voice in this world.

Wilma's humble, strong, and radiant presence graced the bookstore, the church where she gave her reading, and me. I still have the introduction I wrote, slipped into a reading copy of *Every Day Is a Good Day*. The short time we spent together fortified me. I had always admired Wilma, and her life story resonated with me, as it does with so many Native women. She had gracefully negotiated the tough, men-only world of Indian politics. She had raised children on her own, faced trauma and accidents, and lived with cancer. Her life was achingly and personally familiar to us all. Her accomplishments, however, stood alone. For that reason, I had expected to meet someone with a bigger ego or a toughened persona, an edge that she'd certainly had to develop in order to survive.

Instead, in those short hours, I was delighted to walk with a woman of quiet kindness who was genuinely interested in those around her. It was a warm fall day and there were still leaves wafting through the air around us. The people who'd come to the bookstore were proud and excited to meet Wilma. She made everyone feel that they were doing the right thing, pursuing an important course, defining themselves with dignity. All without a hint of schmaltz. It was an every day very good day.

As for this book, it is a fascinating achievement. There is wisdom on every single page. It is a touchstone book, one to keep on your bedside table. A book to reach for when you can't sleep. A companion book filled with the struggles of other Native women. An honest book resonating with humor and survival strategy.

When introducing Wilma Mankiller, I said that she was a representative of our best selves. I didn't just mean Native women, though, I meant everyone. If everyone cared as much about their people, their family, if everyone worked steadfastly for others, if everyone knew that making one's community a better place is an everyday task and you can't let up, yes, we'd live in a more ideal world. But neither Wilma nor any of the women in this book have ever lived there. We live in a frayed and torn world, filled with marvelous opportunities and stunning inequality, a world of shattering blows and sudden loveliness. It takes a greathearted woman to take that all in, and that was Wilma, as greathearted as the voices in this book.

When you take this well-made book into your hands, please feel the heft of voices, the experience, the diversity within the term *Native woman*, and the joy of being who you are, and who we are. All of that lies within, and much more. Lastly, one of Wilma's greatest accomplishments was this: she went home and she made a positive difference. It is true, she left again last year. Again, she went home. To many of us, the sky looks brighter because she's up there still making a positive difference.

—Louise Erdrich, Gakaabiikong (Minneapolis), 2011

foreword

Vine Deloria Jr.

Wilma Mankiller has long been in the forefront of social and political action nationally and in her various communities, be it San Francisco, the Cherokee Nation, or the bewildering number of tribes where she is a welcome and cherished visitor. Her biography, *Mankiller: A Chief and Her People*, chronicles a lifetime of adventures, disappointments, and successes, and above all the determination to go forward regardless of the cost. This attitude of enduring optimism has given strength to the many people who look up to her as an example of a traditional Indian lady.

The old Indian war cry "It's a good day to die" bespoke of the courage and fearlessness of men in battle and indicated that life was not worth living if one approached it with too much caution. Freedom demanded the willingness to sacrifice everything to ensure personal integrity. But what of the long periods between wars and crises? What about the daily lives we seek to fill with substance? Wilma has wisely taken the war cry and shown that Indian women have a spirit that transcends even the commitment to courage and love and holds societies together through the force of deeply cherished personalities. "Every day is a good day," Wilma tells us, and this insight pervades the lives of Indian women who, regardless of the situation they faced, turned hardship into prosperity and created an identity for their people that could not be destroyed.

In this book we have a gathering of minds commenting on the

important issues of the day as only a woman's perspective can help us understand them. Arranged on a topical framework, nineteen women offer their interpretation of such topics as ceremony, governance, womanhood, love and acceptance, and, most importantly, sketch out the need and way to go home. Some comments are long, others short, and not surprisingly represent such a consensus of opinion and experience that we come to recognize the strength that women give to our communities and ourselves. Technical jargon is absent here as the discussion centers on the practical, the well-lived life, not the speculations entertained by lawyers and politicians. Issues are understood in their grassroots applicable context—whatever people might think a concept means, we always see it in our immediate and demanding situation.

The format of this book suggests that the proper way to present history and politics must be biographical history—or perhaps historical biography. Stories count, footnotes inhibit and control. Too much history is written as if the people of any era were just puppets responding to the great issues of the day. Too many of the biographies concentrate on the important events when the course of daily life has provided the context within which people make their decisions, often based on considerations that have little historical meaning but immense and intense concern for the people around us. These selections are a delight to read because they reflect real situations confronted by real people.

Different life experiences characterize each discussion, and it is not difficult to see that one role of women has been to find ways to express abstract ideas in a practical setting, making the changes in policies and programs take a backseat to the more long-term concerns of friends and families. Clearly the family is created and sustained by the mothers and grandmothers, but we can also see the changing roles in which these women have found themselves and how they made adjustments in thinking and behavior that enabled them to always be a source of authority for the community. The transitions these women have made certainly appear to have been smoother than we would expect, although a great deal of remembered pain also resides in their stories.

every day is a good day

The discussions focus on the continuing role each person sees herself playing, and it would not be amiss to say that without the translation of complex problems into solvable activities we could not go forward. Thus the women provide a different function today than they did in the old days, and we can see that everyone's favorite word, "traditional," emerges time and again in new clothes, is accepted by friends and relatives as the proper course of action, different from other times yet applicable today. The readers will find themselves comfortable reading these encounters and yearn for more from each participant. That these interviews are so carefully put together so that real dialog exists is a testament to the real genius Wilma has represented.

The book represents a new form of writing that makes me very enthusiastic. My first reaction to the format was to go through the old treaty minutes and put together a similar dialog between the treaty chiefs and the presidents of the United States so that people could see what might have been the course of action had the tribes been able to express their concerns directly to the president and not suffered the anonymity of having their thoughts summarized by lower-level bureaucrats. This is a book well worth reading and having.

foreword

introduction
wheels over indian trails

Gloria Steinem

This is a very important book. It could be the most important of this new century if it were to get the mindfulness it deserves. Wilma Mankiller has brought together wise voices in a conversation about the things for which we long the most: *Community*, a sense of belonging in the universal scheme of things, support from kin and friends, feeling valued as we are. *Balance*, between people and nature, women and men, youth and age, people of different skills and colors, past and present and future. *Peaceful ways of resolving differences*, sitting in a circle, listening and talking, a consensus that is more important than the time it takes. *Being of good mind*, a positive outlook that energizes positive words and actions. *Circle as paradigm*, a full range of human qualities in each of us, equal value of different tasks, reciprocity, a way of thinking that goes beyond *either/or* and hierarchy. *Spirituality*, the mystery in all living things, the greatest and smallest, and therefore, the origin of balance, a good mind, peace, community.

I suspect we are all drawn to these lifeways. They may be in our DNA from the 95 percent of human history in which they were common, before patriarchy made hierarchy seem natural. I know we are suffering without them. Kids deprived of community create gangs, adults without talking circles create conflict, people without balance "conquer" nature and so defeat themselves, and cultures without spirituality consign it to life after death. Even the liberals and conservatives who are so divided in this country—like the democrats and theocrats who are killing each other in the world—are different only in that liberals and democrats still hope to move toward these possibilities, while conservatives and theocrats consign them to an elite or another life.

Both sides should read this book. They will find evidence that the more than 500 advanced cultures on this continent before Europeans arrived—cultures that often shared values with indigenous groups on other continents—developed wisdom that has been carried on by a few people despite centuries of genocide, theft of homelands, and forced assimilation. Their mission to preserve what is often called The Way is so strong that they are willing to share it with the descendants of invaders who killed 90 percent of their ancestors with war and imported diseases. As Jaune Quick-to-See Smith says in these pages, "Culture is not race and race is not culture." Many traditional women and men feel that the danger of the path we are now on is becoming so great that it no longer can be ignored, that they are guarding The Way on behalf of all the passengers on this fragile Spaceship Earth.

The contemporary indigenous women who speak in these pages—as well as Vine Deloria, a Standing Rock Sioux who is a professor of law, religious and political studies, and the author of important books of his own—are not describing lifeways of the past but ways of thinking and acting that are alive in the present.

You and I who are outsiders to these lifeways—who have lost our path to them on our own ancestral continents—may wonder if they are contrary to history, or even human nature. After all, our history books traditionally started when Europeans arrived, not when people evolved—a difference of 500 years versus tens of thousands. Until the 1960s, many Native Americans were forbidden to teach their own culture and languages in schools or to hold spiritual ceremonies, and their children were forced into Christian boarding schools, as if the separation of church and state didn't exist. Even now, only people who live in

every day is a good day

Indian Country, learn from traditionalists, or study the few but growing number of books like the one you hold in your hands—books that bring indigenous values into the contemporary world or document the past through handed-down stories, archaeology, and such new tools as carbon dating and DNA trails—know much of anything about the people who walked the same land that we do, saw the same mountains, harvested the same waters, and buried their dead in the same earth.

Most of us never learned that they had democratic forms of self-governance before Greece and without slavery, irrigation systems and astronomical calendars as advanced as those of Rome, and medicine using herbs and psychotherapeutic skills when Europe was relying on "humours" and leeches. We didn't know that they domesticated crops that would later save Europe from famine, cherished an oral and sometimes written body of literature, and created trade routes through what are now called Canada, Mexico, Central America, and South America. They were as accustomed to cooperation as we are to competition, as steeped in self-authority as we are in mass persuasion, as used to planning for seven future generations as we are to instant gratification, as daring in exploring inner space as we are in exploring outer space.

I could quote outside authorities on this suppressed history. For example, Benjamin Franklin and other authors of the U.S. Constitution and Bill of Rights used the Iroquois Confederacy as one of their sources. Lewis Henry Morgan, an American ethnologist of the 1800s, documented the self-governance of the six major northeastern tribes by reciprocity, balance, consensus, and communal land ownership. His most famous book, *Ancient Society*, inspired Marx and Engels to aim for these goals, even in the midst of England's brutal class system and industrialization. In 1885, U.S. Senator Henry Dawes was assigned by Congress to report on the Cherokee Nation. Only fifty years after its forced relocation and massive losses on the Trail of Tears, he found that Cherokee cooperation had again created a more literate and prosperous community than the surrounding population, with schools for both girls and boys and "not one pauper in that nation." However, this was seen as a problem. As he

introduction

wrote, "There is no enterprise to make your home any better than your neighbors. There is no selfishness, which is at the bottom of civilization." Therefore, the Dawes Act forced Cherokees to divide their communally owned land into private property.

As for Native women, suffragists regularly cited their status as evidence that women and men could and should have balanced roles. Indeed, there was no other visible source of hope in this New World where expansionism rested on the unpaid labor and uncontrolled reproduction of all women, as well as the outright slavery and forced reproduction of black women and men. In 1888, ethnologist and suffragist Alice Fletcher, who lived among the northeastern tribes, reported to the International Council of Women that "the woman owns her horses, dogs, and all the lodge equipments; children own their own articles; and parents do not control the possessions of their children ... A wife is as independent as the most independent man in our midst." Combined with the fact that among many tribes, female elders chose, advised, and could depose the male chief and signed treaties with the U.S. government along with male leaders—and that women could divorce and controlled their own fertility though a knowledge of herbs and timing—this caused indigenous women to be seen as immoral and tribal systems to be ridiculed as "petticoat government."

As Paula Gunn Allen, Laguna/Sioux poet and novelist, wrote in *The Sacred Hoop: Recovering the Feminine in American Indian Traditions*, "Feminists too often believe that no one has ever experienced the kind of society that empowered women and made that empowerment the basis of rules and civilization. ... the root of oppression is the loss of memory."

This does not mean that "Indian Country"—a term for the diverse Native American community wherever it may be—should be idealized for its equality now. As you will hear from the women in these pages, it has absorbed centuries of male dominance. Yet unlike those of us who know nothing of so-called prehistory, Native women and men have a tradition of balance to bring into the twenty-first century.

Even as someone who comes from what Joy Harjo calls here the

every day is a good day

"overculture," I have sometimes glimpsed this parallel reality. I owe this to the generosity of Native women and men who tolerated and even welcomed someone born on their land, yet raised with no understanding of its history. I'll add a few such stories here to serve as bridges for other outsiders, but I have no explanation for the odd feeling of "home" they give me. Most of all, I owe my sense of old/new possibilities to my friend Wilma Mankiller, whose great heart brings hope to everyone around her, in these pages as in everyday life.

. . .

It is 1977. Twenty thousand women are meeting in Houston for the First National Women's Conference, the culmination of a two-year process of electing delegates and raising issues from every state and territory. Because Bella Abzug and other congresswomen won public funding for this creation of an agenda by and for the female half of the nation, this meeting is probably the most racially and economically representative the country has ever seen. One evidence is the number of women from different Native tribes and nations—in their memory, more than have been able to meet together before. Along with African American, Hispanic, Asian/Pacific American, and other women of color, they are forging a "Minority Women's Plank" to add to a shared agenda.

Time is short before the plenary session will vote, so they have asked me to serve as a "scribe" who collects statements from these caucuses, condenses them into shared themes, then resubmits the result for their approval. I notice that the "American Indian/Alaskan Native" caucus has poetry; indeed, "Earth Mother and the Great Spirit" are the only soaring words anywhere at this conference that is understandably focused on issues and statistics, and "hunting, fishing, and whaling" are the only references to nature. Nobody wants to lose these words, so all the caucuses decide it's okay to append individual paragraphs to the plank, thus uniqueness can coexist with unity. This allows Hispanic women to oppose deporting mothers of U.S.-born children, Asian/Pacific American women to condemn sweatshops—and so on—all because Native women brought their culture with them.

introduction

As I make a last late-night round of caucuses, I notice that exhausted members seem more relaxed, even joyful. By the next day when a spokeswoman from each one reads part of this appended Minority Plank on the floor, their high spirits fill the convention hall. In a moment that delegates and journalists later describe as the high point of the conference, the whole plank is accepted by acclamation.

Afterward, the tribal women give gifts. To this day, I have my blue floral beadwork necklace in the style of the Woodlands people and my red shawl stitched with purple and gold ribbons. I wear the necklace whenever I have to do something especially hard and the shawl whenever I have the chance to dance at a powwow. Still, the most precious gift of all was that moment when 20,000 women became part of one circle.

In later years, I've often thought about this example of being unique, yet part of a community, an alternate to the *either/or* thinking that assumes community must compromise individualism—and vice versa. I notice that some Native parents wait to name a child until she or he does something unique, then add this name to family, clan, and tribe. At powwows, children wear miniature versions of tribal dress, not special designs or colors that would separate them from grown-ups. Everyone's tribe is easily identifiable, yet handmade regalia may be made and worn in an individual way. (Of course, blue jeans, suits, and briefcases are also Native dress, as you'll see in these pages.) In a symbolic system that is rooted in the uniqueness of plants and animals—sage for purification, the bear for motherhood, the eagle for courage, and so on—diversity is linked, not ranked. Ceremonies include a touching reference to "the two-legged and the four-legged," a distinction without a judgment, and invoke "the four directions" and "all our relations," meaning all living things.

Those of us who dwell only in the land of *either/or*—of individualism versus community, humans versus nature—have a lot to learn.

• • •

every day is a good day

Many times a year beginning in the 1980s, I meet with the board of the Ms. Foundation for Women and other groups that now have Native American members. Our meetings always had warmth and an iconoclastic humor, but I notice that they become more so. Whether it's gentle irony about the number of white women who claim descent from "a Cherokee princess" (there was no such thing) or media questions about why Native women aren't wearing tribal regalia (for the same reason European American women aren't wearing bonnets and bustles), there is a humorous way of dealing with the daily realities of racism. From this I learn that humor and seriousness go together; indeed, the more pervasive the injustice, the greater the need for humor.

However, these new members seem bemused by the number of funding requests and discussions about sex education, lesbian rights, eating disorders, and other bodily self-esteem issues for women and girls. They look at us, their European American, African American, and Latina sisters, with kindness, as if we were new arrivals from outer space. Some try to explain that sexuality is just part of life. They illustrate this with stories of courtship and marriage customs, or of grandmothers talking around the kitchen table, or of the special places traditionally allotted to warrior women, nurturing men, and "twin-spirited" people. Others tell stories of riding ponies and playing stickball as part of valuing female bodies for what they can do, not just how they look, and the bumper stickers in Indian Country that say "Brown and Round" in whimsical defiance of a thin-and-white ideal.

I think: This easy humor and earthiness are part of what the New Age idea of Native American life just doesn't get.

I also go to sweat lodge ceremonies and discover that spirituality and humor don't have to be separate either. Prayers come in waves, as may silence or laughter, and all feel as natural together as the people themselves, from the old man seeking help from the spirits in finding a lost horse to the young woman who seeks the strength to survive AIDS. Unlike the walking-on-eggshells feeling of going to a church or temple or mosque, this is a barefoot-on-the-earth feeling of being oneself.

introduction

In the early 1990s, Rebecca Adamson, a Cherokee friend who is the head of First Nations Financial Project, asks if I want to go to a small meeting in the Badlands of South Dakota where activists will try to come up with a new financial paradigm. The idea is to add community and spiritual values to a bottom line that is otherwise only financial. As Rebecca says, "It's economics, with values added."

During this two-day meeting, I notice something almost as amazing as the idea that success isn't just about money: *The men only talk when they have something to say.* For example, an Iroquois man listens for a couple of hours, then gets up to make suggestions and diagrams, then listens again. Not only does he *not* try to control the meeting and *not* try to impress the group, but he is comfortable with silence.

I realize that he has taught me something by its absence: I've been allowing well-meaning men to control meetings *because I'd never experienced any other way.* Of course, I've also seen Native men be as domineering as anybody else, but the point is: I've never seen a *non*-Native man be as comfortable with cooperation, listening, silence.

From this I learn: It's possible.

• • •

I'm not expecting any lessons about indigenous cultures to flow from the bloody break-up of the former Yugoslavia during the 1990s. In the service of ethnic hierarchy, neighbors are killing neighbors, long intermarried families are taking sides against their own kin, and rape has become a weapon of ethnic cleansing. This is all supposed to be justified as retribution for violence of generations ago.

But as Wilma and other wise friends point out, that *is* the lesson: They have forgotten the experience of Native Americans here, the Kwei and the San in Africa, and perhaps the indigenous tribes that roamed Eastern Europe millennia ago: *One act of violence takes four generations to heal.* One may choose violence when there seems no other way, but not without understanding the cost. It is the very opposite of the modern idea that violence *ends* violence.

It occurs to me that the superimposition of Marxism only brought another layer of forgetfulness of indigenous values. Marx and Engels may have been inspired by the "primitive communism" of the Iroquois Confederacy, but they ignored the principle that violence was likely to create more violence, that the means dictate the ends. Indeed, they preached the contrary: The end justifies the means. Marxism used all the worthwhile goals of indigenous life to justify almost any means. In a way, this is also the opposite of the logic of the Good Mind that Audrey Shenandoah explains in these pages. It justifies the negative and angry mind.

From this I learn the danger of all who would appropriate Native life: Lifting an element of The Way from its lived context can be a risky thing.

• • •

It is the mid-1990s, and I've been asked to speak about cooperative classroom styles that are helping girls learn and providing alternatives to competition for some boys, too. The occasion is a national conference of Native American educators who use Native history to teach engineering, chemistry, astronomy, mathematics, and other fields—areas that Native students are otherwise made to feel they do not "own." I'm going on faith because Wilma suggested it, and because she will be speaking, too.

I'm to be met at the airport in Detroit, but I see no one except a heavyset man in a windbreaker who is leaning against the wall. He doesn't move in my direction. When no one else shows up, I ask if he is waiting for me—and he is.

I make small talk in the car by asking what he does for this huge conference. He says mildly that he is the head of it. He would have been content to continue being the driver if I hadn't asked; so much for hierarchy. As we pass a turn-off sign that says "Serpent Mound," I ask what it is. Instead of being surprised that I, who grew up in this area, don't know, he just explains that it is an important example of hundreds of indigenous earthworks scattered across this subcontinent. They testify to the burial customs, astronomical knowledge, and lifeways of cultures at least a millennia before Columbus and often contain tools and jewelry

introduction

made of bones or stone sheathed in hammered copper, decorations studded with freshwater pearls, remnants of pottery, woven cloth, and objects that could only have come from faraway trade. Indeed, some of these mounds may have taken centuries to build—with thousands of pounds of earth moved to create them, and the resulting basins turned into lakes for fish hatcheries. Until fairly recently, many authorities assumed such earthworks could not have been created by ancestors of the "primitive" peoples on this subcontinent, thus one of the Lost Tribes of Israel must have lived here in prehistory. Indeed, Mormons are still teaching this.

"I have friends who went to see Stonehenge in England," he says. "I asked them if they wouldn't like to see monuments here that are older and just as meaningful. They said no."

That's it. Somehow this "no" combines with my own ignorance as it has come home to me over the last twenty years and becomes the last straw. While my host is still smiling with the irony of their response, I am feeling angrier and more impatient, as if such emotions have been piling up and are finally spilling over.

I promise myself that I will spend what I can of the rest of my life making up for this lack of a knowledge that we may be literally dying for: not only of those mound-builders, or the Midwest settlement the size of London before Columbus showed up, or the southwestern tribes whose cliff dwellings have only recently been seen from helicopters—but also the modern Native novelists and poets and filmmakers who create with the double vision of what is and what could be, the tribes fighting against methane extraction and nuclear waste to save their land and our environment, the urban centers and colleges where Native cultures flower in the midst of skyscrapers, the new hope of "re-tribalizing" in an age when technology allows people to gather without nationalism or hierarchy—and most of all, the chance to listen to the voices of indigenous women whose living version of The Way I have been glimpsing over three decades.

When I say this to Wilma, she smiles, as if I've arrived in a place she already knows. She has been planning to travel around the country, to talk with indigenous women leaders who are so busy holding the world together that they have little time to strengthen each other's spirits, and to create a conversation that will support them and pass their wisdom on.

That was a decade ago. This is the living conversation you hold in your hands.

• • •

At the beginning of this journey years ago, I came home from road trips and saw on the rocks over New York's Midtown Tunnel this huge graffiti: WHEELS OVER INDIAN TRAILS.

I loved these painted words because they made me think: Who had walked across this same island? Who had touched the same outcroppings of igneous rock? Who had crossed the same rivers and looked out from the same ocean shore? Who had lived on the land where my house is built over an underground river, at the edge of a timeless boulder that stretches all the way to the center of the island?

I came to call this vertical history more visceral, sensory, and anchored in the land than the horizontal version that disappears into the mists of time. Still, I assumed that "Indian trails" meant the past and "wheels" meant the present.

Now, I wonder if the writer of this graffiti meant something different. After all, trails and wheels cover the same land and could be guided by the same wisdom.

These lifeways could be the wheels that will carry us all.

introduction

the gathering

Preface

Nowhere is the Haudenosaunee
appreciation for women better reflected than
in their music and dance. When the women
dance, they form a circle around the drum;
they move with the Earth, counterclock-
wise, their feet caressing the Earth as they
shuffle to one of the hundreds of verses
sung in their honor. To be part of that circle
is a great source of strength for me.
—Joanne Shenandoah

When indigenous women gather in our homes, at ceremonial grounds, or at meetings, our conversations are often quite different from those with non-Native people. Not only do we often speak about different things, we speak about them in an entirely different way. This gathering of women is a rare opportunity for outsiders to sit in on the candid conversations of indigenous women as they speak about love, life, their families, and their communities.

The conversations with the nineteen women at this gathering were held in separate places, from Onondaga Territory to Hawai'i, but their comments are organized into a larger discussion in an effort to invoke the sense of a gathering. No matter where indigenous women gather or for what purpose, they almost always talk about family and community and express concern about traditional values, culture, and lifeways slipping away. It is the women who are responsible for bringing along the next generation to carry the culture forward. The extended family, clan, community, and nation are the significant universe for the women at this gathering, and they speak about issues within the context of family and community. Family is described in terms of an extensive kinship system of relationships with people who are not always related by blood.

Community is not always a specific geographic space shared by people with common interests and values; it is sometimes a larger community of culture in which people share values and a sense of responsibility for one another. In urban areas, Native people from diverse tribal nations do not always have their own physical community, but they maintain a strong community of culture, of relationships, of shared experiences and kinship. Many regularly travel back and forth to their homelands for spiritual, social, and cultural sustenance. They have also built impressive Indian centers and friendship houses in urban areas to provide services, socialize, and hold meetings and cultural events. But no matter how long Native people live away, many continue to derive their identity from their homelands. One could ask a Sicangu Lakota woman whose family has lived in an urban area for several generations where she is from, and she will respond, "I am from Rosebud," or wherever her homelands may be.

The oral history, discussion, vignettes, and stories that follow are not comprehensive in nature and do not preach a certain doctrine. Neither the women at this gathering nor I purport to speak for others or for all indigenous women. The conversations provide a snapshot of a xxix

small, diverse group of women who made a conscious choice to lead a meaningful life by building on the positive attributes of their communities instead of focusing only on the daunting set of economic and social problems that they deal with daily. They find many moments of grace, beauty, and joy in their busy lives. Despite everything, they tend to view economic poverty as a barrier and a challenge, not a state of being.

The unusual format of this book came out of a conversation with Alice Walker. When I mentioned my interest in interviewing Native women to her, she recommended reading John Langston Gwaltney's *Drylongso: A Self-Portrait of Black America*. The African American people interviewed in that book speak about issues and events in their lives in a very honest, straightforward way. They would never have been that open with an outsider. With *Drylongso* in mind, I had the idea that the women I interviewed would engage in very frank discussion with me because we share a common heritage, many life experiences, and values. In addition to their voices, each chapter begins with an essay to provide some historical background and context to make the discussions more meaningful to people who may know very little about indigenous women. Then a personal story from my life is shared as a prelude to the conversation, just as is often the case when women gather.

It was extraordinarily difficult to separate the material into chapters and protect the integrity of the discussion. These women do not live their lives in a segmented way and do not speak about a single issue as if it were separate from the whole. I made no attempt to structure the comments of the women into relatively equal length. In all discussions, some people are more apt to listen and only occasionally contribute to the conversation, while others speak eloquently for extended periods of time. Such is the case here. Some women had more to say on one subject than another, and others made no comment at all on some subjects. The comments of Mary and Carrie Dann appear together because their words flowed together seamlessly. Florence Soap, whose remarks were translated from Cherokee into English, only offered remarks on a couple of issues.

Though the women at this gathering are quite diverse, they share

preface

a number of common values and characteristics, including a sense of duty and responsibility to others, tremendous tenacity, and an unwillingness to ever, ever give up. Audrey Shenandoah finds the concept of burnout completely incomprehensible. She said, "I don't know what being burned out means. I can understand being tired, but after having a peaceful night of rest, everything is okay again. I am always thankful for the things I still can do. I have a great feeling of caring for my community. My community isn't just here at Onondaga. It is the Haudenosaunee and all the people all over the land." I hope that in the following pages people from many different communities "all over the land" will learn something of value about the special world in which these women live their lives and conduct their work with such dignity, faith, hope, and optimism.

We pray for all life: spirit life,
human life, animal life, insect life.
All life is included in seasonal ceremonies.
—Mary and Carrie Dann
(Western Shoshone)

every day is a good day

acknowledgments

There is nothing I can say or do to adequately express my deep gratitude to my niece Virlee Williamson for donating a kidney and stem cells to me. When I was undergoing kidney dialysis treatments, I never prayed for a long life. I prayed for a little space without treatments or major medical trauma. Virlee has generously provided me with that space.

Special thanks to Charlie Soap, who provided love, encouragement, and most of the photographs, and to Bob Friedman and Kristina Kiehl, who taught me the true nature of unconditional friendship and trust. *Wa-do* to Gloria Steinem for inspiration and thoughtful feedback and to Michael Chapman, who learned a lot about female leadership and reciprocity from his mother, Lucille Chapman. Jaune Quick-to-See Smith also took time from her busy schedule to make a number of very helpful comments. My daughters, Felicia and Gina, organized the manuscript and transcribed all the conversations. The Lannon and Kellogg Foundations provided fellowships that enabled me to devote the time necessary to complete this project. I am deeply appreciative of the support of Sam Scinta, Faith Marcovecchio, Ann Douden, and all the people at Fulcrum Publishing who worked with me on every aspect of this book in a spirit of genuine partnership.

contributors

My deep gratitude to the women
who participated in this project.

Linda Aranaydo, Muscogee Creek (physician)

Mary and Carrie Dann, Western Shoshone (traditionalists)

Angela Gonzales, Hopi (professor)

Joy Harjo, Muscogee Creek/Cherokee (poet/musician)

LaDonna Harris, Comanche (warrior)

Sarah James, Nee'Tsaii Gwich'in (human rights activist)

Debra LaFountaine, Ojibway (environmentalist)

Rosalie Little Thunder, Lakota (Lakota linguist/artist)

Lurline Wailana McGregor, Native Hawaiian
(television producer)

Beatrice Medicine, Lakota (anthropologist)

Ella Mulford, Navajo (biologist)

Jaune Quick-to-See Smith, Salish Flathead (artist)

Audrey Shenandoah, Onondaga (Clan Mother)

Joanne Shenandoah, Oneida (musician)

*Gail Small (Head Chief Woman), Northern Cheyenne
(environmental activist)*

Faith Smith, Ojibway (educator)

Florence Soap, Cherokee (grandmother)

Octaviana Valenzuela Trujillo, Pascua Yaqui (educator)

contributors

harvest moon

Chapter One

The medicine man arrived at our rural Oklahoma home on a cool fall day during that soft time just before dusk. As he busied himself gathering material for the evening ceremony in the woods surrounding our house, the Maple led the trees in a final burst of yellow and orange. Soon the nourishing rains would come to wash the leaves to the earth as part of an endless cycle of renewal. It was a good time for ceremony: a time of changing seasons, transition, and new beginnings. A time once called Harvest Moon, when Cherokee people gathered for ceremonies to mark the end of the growing seasons and the beginning of a new year.

When the Sun settled in the west, my family, friends, and I quieted our minds, opened our hearts, and began the ceremony. It was called to help me recover from my own "perfect storm" of chemotherapy treatments, political strife, and family trauma and to provide me with the strength to face additional medical treatments and an uncertain future. That night of prayer, songs, and ceremony took an unexpected turn when the medicine man planted the seed for this book by giving me and my daughter Gina special medicine to enable us to help tell the stories of others.

When the ceremony was over at dawn we all faced east to greet the new morning with a sense of renewal in our hearts, and the secrets we whispered during the ceremony safely tucked away. Besides my immediate family, two extraordinary women joined me for the ceremony, Debra LaFountaine, an Ojibway woman who always leads with heart, and Roberta Manuelito, who learned traditional Navajo ways from her beloved grandfather. By the time everyone began their journey home with their spirits still warmly wrapped in the ceremonial songs of the previous night, I was thinking about ways to share the experiences of women such as Roberta and Debra who get up every morning and stand for something larger than themselves.

Besides Debra and Roberta, many incredible women have danced in and out of my life. They are grandmothers, mothers, daughters, aunts, lovers, friends, sisters, and partners. Some have buried husbands and children, faced racism, confronted daunting health problems, and dealt with a staggering set of problems caused by extreme economic poverty, yet they lead their nations, their families, and their communities with dignity, strength, and optimism. Justine Buckskin was such a woman. She came to mind when I heard the Mohawk proverb, "It is hard to see the future with tears in your eyes." She faced great hardship in her life but didn't have time for despair. She kept a steady gaze toward the future. When I was an impressionable eleven-year-old, Justine invited me into her life by offering a babysitting job. I took the job, and we remained friends for the next four decades. Justine served on every board even remotely connected to the San Francisco Bay Area Native American community. She was a one-woman social service agency, the most relentlessly positive woman I have ever met. Even when she was down on her luck, she found a way to help others who were in worse circumstances. She had a gift for focusing on the positive attributes of people in difficult situations. When others saw only rough edges on me and the other youth who frequented the San Francisco Indian Center, Justine saw potential leaders and professionals. It was Justine who encouraged me to go to college and then accompanied me to campus to make sure I enrolled. Sadly, Justine was so busy taking care of other people that she did not always take care of herself. She developed diabetes. And when her kidneys failed she had to undergo dialysis, and then poor circulation caused the amputation of an arm. When I last saw her in San Francisco in the winter of 1990, she was quite frail, yet she spoke passionately about her work in the community and as a volunteer at Highland Hospital in Oakland, where she was helping other amputees learn how to live independently, as she always had. When people ask me what women influenced me, I always talk about Justine. Someone once told me that the Earth will always remember people as long as we continue to say their name. I often say Justine Buckskin's name.

Audrey Shenandoah, an Onondaga Clan Mother, also comes to mind. Her powerful message of peace and hope has inspired thousands of people throughout the world. Out of love, respect, and concern for her people, she teaches the Onondaga language and the ways of the Haudenosaunee (People of the Longhouse) to children and members of her community. As a Clan Mother she is responsible for the welfare and social harmony of the clan. She gives traditional Onondaga names to people of the clan and has an important role in the installation and removal of male chiefs, who are considered Caretakers of the Peace.

Mary and Carrie Dann represent the personification of indigenous womanhood—beautiful, strong, loving, free women who live full, rich lives with their children and grandchildren while waging a forty-year battle to keep the U.S. government from impounding their horses and cattle and evicting them from their land. Now grandmothers themselves, they learned traditional Western Shoshone ways and values from their own grandmother, who would have been so proud to know her granddaughters would stare down the United States government for more than four decades to protect Shoshone lands.

While the U.S. government was preparing to invade Iraq to "fight terrorism," the Bureau of Land Management sent military-style convoys to round up hundreds of heads of cattle and horses belonging to Mary and Carrie Dann. The Dann sisters called the raids "domestic terrorism" with good reason. The government has fined the Dann sisters more than $2 million for grazing fees, interest, and penalties on what it claims is U.S. government land. It is difficult to understand why there has not been more of a public outcry against the federal government for raiding Shoshone land to confiscate the horses and cattle, and for trying to break the spirit and resolve of two elder Shoshone women.

The Western Shoshone never lost their land in war, by congressional act, or by treaty. Yet the U.S. government has taken the incomprehensible position that the Western Shoshone lost their land in 1872 to settlers who "gradually encroached" on the land, ostensibly ending Shoshone land rights. Mary Dann says, "We've repeatedly asked the federal government for Western Shoshone land transfer documents. If our ancestors agreed to give up or sell this land, we would respect the government. But the federal agencies have never been able to show us any document giving away the land. This is still our homeland." The position of the Dann sisters has been supported by a majority of Western Shoshone Tribal Councils, the National Congress of American Indians, and the Organization of American States, as well as dozens of global organizations and thousands of individuals.

Despite the decades-long fight waged by the Western Shoshone, the U.S. Congress recently passed legislation they allege extinguishes Shoshone title to the land and opens the land up for mining. Western Shoshone lands are the third-largest gold producing area in the world. The Western Shoshone Distribution Bill, signed by President Bush on July 7, 2004, purports to take tens of millions of acres of Shoshone land for payment of $145 million, most of which will be paid to thousands of eligible tribal members. Some of the funds will be used to set up an educational fund. But even with the passage of the distribution bill, the Dann sisters and other Western Shoshone have vowed to never give up the fight to retain their homelands, and say they will join many other tribal members in refusing to accept any payment for their land. Carrie Dann says, "I'm not going to sell my dignity, my spirituality, my culture. No way. I'm looking at the future of our children. I'm looking at our birthright, which is not for sale for $20,000."

There are many other women who have had an impact on me, including all the women whose conversations are included in this book.

I am privileged to have close friendships with women from many cultures and economic backgrounds with whom I share common interests, though we live very different lives. But my relationships with indigenous women, particularly those who synchronize their lives with the land and the community, are markedly different from my relationships with most of my other friends. The deep, binding connection among indigenous women can be explained in part by our common life experiences, patterns of thought, and shared values, but I also believe it can be partially explained by a more complete, whole, interconnected understanding of the world. Among these women, there is less of a tendency to organize everything into categories and segments than there is in the larger society. While many of my other friends describe objects or events in a way that detaches them from their context, my tradition-oriented indigenous friends tend to think about, describe, and view things in their totality. They conduct their work and live their lives within the context of the family, clan, community, nation, and universe. Context is everything. They also seem to have a much greater degree of tolerance for the unevenness, differences, and contradictions in life, or what Linda Aranaydo calls "life's backward- and forwardness."

Another factor that greatly contributes to a different view of the world is our identity as members of a culturally distinct group of people with whom we have reciprocal relationships. Joanne Shenandoah says, "It is a beautiful thing to be part of a collective society and community where we are safe. Ingrained in our soul are lessons about our place in the community."

Indigenous women are not only responsible for continuing time-honored traditions, they are also creators and interpreters of indigenous culture in the early twenty-first century, a time when advanced technology draws the entire world closer together and there are many attempts to homogenize world cultures. As native women work for the benefit of future generations, they are embraced by the memory of their ancestors. In the strength of that embrace, the line between the past, present, and future is not as distinct as it is in the larger society. Native women know the sacred places generations of their people have gone for renewal and for ceremony. They know where great battles were once fought and where their people held meetings to discuss momentous decisions about war and peace. They have a special relationship with the land where their ancestors sang their songs, told their stories, and were returned to the earth for burial. This is their homeland.

Outsiders are always admonishing Native women to forget about history and the past, but history is woven into the very fabric of their daily lives. History is much more than a series of abstract events. Gail Small says, "At our Northern Cheyenne homelands we look at history quite differently. Our history is the premise of who we are and how we make decisions today. Each time we hear stories about what American soldiers did to our people, especially our grandmothers, the pain and anger is fresh and raw. What we have gone through is so real, it is like it happened yesterday."

White anthropologists and "experts" on Native Americans have written volumes about the culture of traditional indigenous people with little understanding of the degree to which tribal knowledge continues to inform contemporary Native life. Too many books about specific tribal groups have been written by people who spent fifteen minutes on a reservation and became experts. But that is changing. Native scholars such as Dr. Bea Medicine have written and lectured extensively about the need for greater understanding of indigenous cultures. She said, "White people don't understand us or the strength and diversity of aboriginal people, and they don't even try. That's why there is such racism and misunderstanding. In any kind of reconciliation movement, they expect the Indian people to reconcile with them, and not the other way around." It is almost impossible for an outsider to grasp the underlying values of the community or the culture and lifeways of the people and their relationship to the natural world. Without an intellectual and spiritual frame of reference related to community and an understanding of the extended kinship system, they tend to filter everything through their own lens of the modern nuclear family, distant from the land and often from themselves. If one has never seen a grandmother who was prohibited from speaking her own language in a government boarding school overcome with love and joy when a young child proudly says a few words in her own language, how can one understand the people? If one has never felt the powerful unifying force of an indigenous-language prayer in ceremony, how can one possibly claim to understand indigenous people? Native people who can still speak their indigenous language are well respected. Darrell Kipp, founder of the Nizipuhwahsin Language Immersion School on the Blackfeet Reservation, says, "When people relearn their language, the first thing they wish to do is pray in it."

The movement of indigenous people in and out of two often very different cultures can sometimes cause outsiders to draw erroneous conclusions about the degree of assimilation in a given community. Indigenous people have long understood how to move in and out of parallel universes and maintain their cultural values. Dr. Bea Medicine says, "It is difficult to try to compartmentalize our lives. We have learned to assess the social situation and act accordingly. And it's not schizophrenia; it's just simply a rule to discern the proper behavior in different roles of life."

The pervasive influence of American popular culture has had a dramatic impact on indigenous communities, but it would be folly to draw conclusions about the degree of assimilation in these communities based primarily on external appearances and the fact that indigenous people do not look and act as they did 300 years ago. In tradition-oriented families, young people may watch MTV and older people tune in to CNN, but they filter the information through their own view of the world, which may be quite different from their white neighbors' view. One of my favorite scenes is the family campgrounds at the annual Crow Fair Celebration and Powwow at Crow Agency, Montana, where the dancers and horses are adorned with exquisite beadwork for the parade past dozens of tipis to the powwow grounds. Young people stroll through the powwow grounds with cell phones hooked to their waistbands, and Foreman grills and DVD players sit outside some tipis. I have yet to see a satellite dish in front of a tipi, but it wouldn't surprise me. The juxtaposition of tribal traditions and pop culture sometimes confounds outsiders who seem to think one precludes the other.

Jaune Quick-to-See Smith describes the capriciousness of appearance: "In my art and life, I really strive to reverse the old adage that what you see is what you get. If I can be Coyote and practice my sneak-up, I can engage the viewers from a distance with one image and lure them in for exposure to another layer, which changes the initial view into quite a different reality. After all, that is what ethnic culture is all about—or even an ongoing relationship. What you see on the surface is never the same again once you begin to plumb the depths."

Most people know very little about indigenous women, except for a few almost mythical icons such as Sacajawea, an intelligent, resourceful Shoshone interpreter who accompanied the Lewis and Clark expedition in the early nineteenth century. This appalling lack of accurate information about indigenous women fuels negative stereotypes. Television, film, and print media often portray indigenous women as asexual drudges or innocent children of nature, while rail-thin white women are held up as idealized representations of compassion, beauty, and sexuality. In film, as in the larger society, the power, strength, and complexity of indigenous women are rarely acknowledged or recognized.

While the role of indigenous women in the family and community, now and in the past, differs from nation to nation, each of the women at this gathering stated unequivocally that there was a point in time when there was greater equity between men and women, and that balance between men and women must be restored if we are ever to have whole, healthy communities again. Lurline Wailana McGregor says, "In the past, men and women had very specific roles that complemented each other, assuring a functional and thriving community life. Although these roles are less rigid today, they are no longer balanced. Western cultures devalue women. So now we struggle for equity in the workplace and recognition in our own communities."

Navajo women once controlled the economy by owning and managing the livestock, and Ojibway women trapped small animals, dressed furs, and built canoes. In some indigenous communities, women chose lives that transcended gender roles. Historian Connie Evans described a trader's observation that a Gros Ventre woman dressed as a woman but sat on the council and ranked as the third leading warrior in a band of 180 lodges. She eventually took four wives.

Women have played a significant role in Cherokee society for a very long time. In the distant past, Cherokee people believed that the world existed in a precarious balance and that only right or correct actions maintained that balance. An important part of the balance was equity between men and women. Women were consulted in matters of importance to the community, the clan, the family, and the nation. When a man married a woman, he took up residence with the clan of his wife. Cherokee people trace their clan ancestry through women. There once was a women's council composed of women of each of the seven Cherokee clans. A special woman served as the chief beloved woman, or Ghighau. Female warriors, called War Women or Pretty Women, were tribal dignitaries. There was a belief that the Great Spirit sent messages through women. A woman's power was considered so great that special women were able to declare whether punishment or pardon was to be inflicted upon those who offended the mandate to engage in only right or correct actions.

From the time of European contact, there has been a concerted attempt to diminish the role of indigenous women. But even with the sustained efforts by the federal government and various religious groups to totally assimilate them, women continue to play a critical role in many indigenous communities in formal and informal leadership positions in every sector of tribal society and the larger culture around them.

ceremony

Chapter Two

Spiritualism is the highest form of political consciousness.

—Haudenosaunee message to the world

The spiritual life of indigenous people has been studied, copied, parodied, and exploited, but it has rarely been understood. Some indigenous spiritual practices, such as the Ghost Dance, the Sun Dance, and the Stomp Dance, were once outlawed, forcing the ceremonies to be performed in secret. Despite several hundred years of sustained opposition from the U.S. government and various dogmatic religious groups, the spiritual lifeways, practices, and traditions given to indigenous people by the Creator at the beginning of time continue in round houses, longhouses, kivas, ceremonial grounds, and other sacred places, as well as in their daily lives. Tribal people have tenaciously fought to maintain their traditional lifeways and value systems.

Various Christian groups sent legions of missionaries to convert tribal people, often by separating children from their families in religious boarding schools. Long before the current international scandal regarding

Catholic priests sexually abusing children, in tribal communities there were many stories of extreme physical and sexual abuse at religious Indian boarding schools. Gail Small says, "Children were sexually molested by priests and nuns. Then they came home and spread the cancer themselves." Ojibway educator Faith Smith describes her experience at a mission school as follows: "For a while I attended a mission school, and that was the first time I had ever seen people so white. They were just kind of glowing. They used to wear black habits and it was almost like this iridescent whiteness in the middle of all that black material. And they were the meanest, nastiest people in the world. They would use a ruler or strap on us to punish us for all kinds of stuff. Their behavior seemed peculiar since they always talked with us about the values of Christianity." Rosalie Little Thunder describes herself as a recovering Catholic who has undergone the painful process of healing from her indoctrination at a Catholic boarding school.

Though indigenous people now embrace a wide range of spiritual practices from Christianity to Buddhism, many continue to value tribal knowledge systems and spirituality and often turn to their own indigenous spiritual beliefs for solutions to contemporary problems. Some people attend the church of their choice and also participate in traditional tribal ceremonies. Linda Aranaydo says, "Spirituality is not exclusive, and I don't have a label for it. I feel comfortable going to any place where people go to pray, where people are meditating, where they are going inside themselves to be quiet for a while and listen to life, or where they are being together to comfort one another in a sacred way." Jaune Quick-to-See Smith says, "Praying is like gaining supernatural power outside yourself, a power beyond what you can control."

She continues, "I had always wondered why my family or my tribe weren't conflicted over having the Catholic Church involved in their lives when traditional religion fit our needs even better. That is, until my Aunt Ida was on her last journey and called for both the priest and a medicine person from the longhouse to give her last rites and attend her bedside. During that time I overheard my Uncle Fred casually

every day is a good day

say that Aunt Ida did the right thing. It's like double indemnity insurance. Having prayers from both religions gave my Aunt Ida extra power to make sure her journey went smoothly. Later, in doing some reading of old Salish manuscripts, I discovered that was why the priests were invited to our communities in the mid-1800s. In hunting on our old grounds east of the Rockies, my tribe was constantly being attacked by tribes pushed there by the *Suyapi* (white European) invasion. They had guns and we didn't have them yet. Our people were seeking additional protective power—double indemnity insurance. The flash of understanding hit me about why it might be helpful to have an eagle feather in one hand and a Bible in the other. It can't hurt."

Because of the dearth of accurate information about Native people, stereotypes persist, particularly with regard to spirituality. The myth of a universal Native American spirituality that can be codified into dogmatic religious teachings is dreamed up and perpetuated by self-designated, "medicine people." Traditional spiritual practices hold endless fascination for outsiders who either view them as hopelessly pagan or as singular, mystical events without context. Outsiders sometimes focus on and even try to replicate discrete practices or ceremonies of traditional tribal groups, with little attempt to understand the complex belief systems and lifeways they represent. Adorned with crystal and turquoise or freshly smudged with cedar and sage, earnest non–Native Americans seek out indigenous leaders for spiritual guidance. Others perform the sacred Sun Dance as a public event. As Lakota scholar Bea Medicine points out, "they don't have all the information they need to properly perform these ceremonies." In the absence of knowledge about their own spiritual values and instructions about how to have peace of mind, live with one another, and co-exist with the land, outsiders turn to indigenous spiritual leaders hoping for an easy set of instructions in "Native American spirituality" to help them understand themselves and their place in an excessively self-indulgent society devoid of spirituality. Gail Small adds, "In ancient times white people probably also had an understanding that everything was connected. They have lost their culture.

ceremony

They had to leave their land and move to a new continent. It would be almost impossible to keep their culture intact. There are only a few ancient cultures, such as the Chinese, that have come here and been able to maintain their culture." Gail continues: "We view life here on Earth as a very short journey. We are not driven by the need to accumulate material things or by greed. In the American way of thinking, their daily life and their church and spirituality are fractionated and distinctly different. Whereas, among the Cheyenne, everything is centered on the Creator. All human beings are like one small spoke in a big wheel of Creation. There is no hierarchy, and the Creator is at the center of the wheel." Joanne Shenandoah echoes this sentiment: "Their society is based on ownership, control, division. They focus on the outer self, while our people focus on the inner self."

Though there are significant cultural differences among the more than 500 distinct tribal groups in the United States, among traditional people there is a fundamental understanding that everything is related and that all living things play an important role in keeping the Earth in balance. Each community derives its unique spiritual and cultural identity from shared values, knowledge, stories, and relationships with one other and the natural world.

Traditional indigenous knowledge systems and stories acknowledge that the rivers, rocks, trees, plant life, and celestial world are alive with spirit and meaning. When traditional indigenous people speak of their relatives, they are referring to every living thing, not just human kinship. The very identity of traditional tribal people is derived from the natural world, the land, and the community. They understand their own insignificance in the totality of things.

The Creator provided us with ceremonies to remind us of our place in the universe and our responsibilities as human beings. In the past, Cherokee people gathered once a year for the recitation of ancient laws given to them by the Creator. These laws, sometimes recorded on wampum belts, gave people guidance on how to properly conduct their lives. Crimes large and small—except murder—were forgiven at this annual ceremony. Everyone who participated in the ceremony was forgiven for past offenses. No one left the ceremony with grudges or animosity toward another. It was a time of renewal and forgiveness.

There are hundreds of different seasonal ceremonies among the diverse tribal groups in North America. Many acknowledge or even mirror certain functions of the natural world or members of animal nations. Each spring, the Northern Ute hold a Bear Dance to shake off the effects of the long winter and prepare them for what lies ahead. The Cherokee have a Green Corn Ceremony to celebrate the ripening of the corn. The Cherokee people's ancient relatives, the Haudenosaunee, hold annual green bean, strawberry, maple, and seed blessing ceremonies, and some of the people of the North Country hold wild-rice ceremonies. The Gwich'in people, who live farther north, believe that the heart of each caribou contains some human heart, and that each human heart contains a bit of caribou heart. According to Sarah James, "The caribou is not just what we eat, but who we are. It is in our dances, stories, songs, and the whole way we see the world. Caribou is how we get from one year to the other." Audrey Shenandoah says, "We have a big ceremony mid-wintertime during the winter solstice when certain people renew their medicine. Some ceremonies, such as the Mask Society, were here even before people were here. Peace of mind is paramount in our ways, in both healing and in thanksgiving. When sick people are given medicine or have a ceremony, it is to bring about peace of mind. The curing is left to the Creator. If they are going to get better right away, we are thankful, but if it is something that will not heal quickly or that they will have for the rest of their lives, peace of mind will help them heal and deal with it. If people do their thanksgiving faithfully, earnestly, and in a humble way, then they will have peace of mind. If they do it in a bragging way, just to show off, that's not good. They have to be humble and respectful in their thanksgiving."

It is a miracle that this knowledge and interconnected view of the world has survived. The most powerful country in the world has made numerous attempts to totally eradicate this worldview, first by war and then later by a plethora of federal policies designed to destroy tribal lifeways. Each time a traditional Cheyenne man engages in a Sun Dance or a Cherokee woman straps on terrapin shells and steps out into the circle to dance, it is practically a revolutionary act, a miracle, a living testament to the enduring spiritual strength of the people.

The women at this gathering steadfastly honor the traditions and belief systems given to their people by the Creator while acknowledging and dealing with considerable challenges. They each deal with a set of severe social and economic problems in their communities, but they hold the people close to their hearts, praying, working, and drawing on their spiritual beliefs for sustenance and support. None of the women try to endlessly analyze or dissect spirituality. They express spirituality through the very way they live their lives. There is no separation between the secular and the sacred. Everything in life is sacred.

Wilma Mankiller

During my childhood my family was not involved in any type of regular religious services or activities, though we did occasion-ally attend one of the small community churches near our rural Adair County, Oklahoma, home or participate in Cherokee Stomp Dances. Though I certainly do not consider myself a spiritual person, I have always been attracted to people of faith. Like Linda Aranaydo, I just "like to be around people who pray." By and large, people of faith, however they express their religious beliefs, seem to be concerned with the question of what it means to be a good person, an issue I have wrestled with.

When Cherokee people lived in our old country in the Southeast, there was little ambiguity about what it meant to be a good person. Everyone had clearly defined roles, and the rules of conduct governing right and correct actions were understood. A good person was prudent in relationships with others and conducted his or her affairs with honor, respect, and dignity. Each year one Cherokee ceremony in a series was conducted in each settlement for the explicit purpose of rekindling relationships, requesting forgiveness for inappropriate conduct during the previous year, and cleansing the minds of Cherokee people of any negative thoughts toward others. One can detect elements of this ceremony in contemporary Cherokee life when the following prayer is recited at the beginning of a gathering: "First, let us remove all negative thoughts from our minds so we can come together as one … "The primary goal of prayer is to promote a sense of oneness and unity. Negative thoughts were treated by Cherokee healers with the same medicines as wounds, headaches, or physical illness. It was believed that unchecked negative thoughts can permeate the being and manifest themselves in negative actions.

I personally experienced the power of a ceremony to remove negative thoughts when I was working for Chief Ross Swimmer in the early 1980s. Several of his senior staff opposed me and created every conceivable barrier to my community development work. Eventually my feelings of resentment toward the leader of this group generated a wide range of unwelcome emotions; I spoke to a Cherokee medicine man about the problem. He arranged a beautiful ceremony at dawn, which helped cleanse my mind, put the actions of my opponents in perspective, and enabled me to continue to work with them in a good way.

When my daughters, Felicia and Gina, and I returned to Oklahoma in the summer of 1976, I began to understand and acknowledge the spiritual dimensions of my life. We had left California with no sense of what was ahead of us. We just knew it was time to go home. When we arrived in Oklahoma, one of the first things we did was visit my old family place that my family had so reluctantly left twenty years earlier. My childhood home had burned down, and the yard and garden were overgrown with foliage, underbrush, and trees. And yet the memories were so strong, I could still clearly see my home.

The Mankiller family land defined who I am. During the period when Indian Territory was dissolved and Oklahoma became a state, the federal government attempted to destroy the Cherokee Nation by dividing up our commonly held land into individual allotments of 160 acres. The family land was allotted to my grandfather, John (Yona) Mankiller, and passed down to my father, Charley Mankiller, and my Aunt Sally Leach. I am grateful that my father rejected offers to sell the land even in the very lean times our family faced after the Bureau of Indian Affairs relocated us to San Francisco. The land held deep memories of my family and the first ten years of my life. During my early childhood, my siblings and I gathered water from a cold spring where my grandparents had also stored melons, fresh milk, and butter. We shared that spring with bobcats, mountain lions, wild pigs, and an occasional deer. With a watchful eye for snakes, we turned over rocks looking for crawdads in the icy water. The banks of the spring were covered with a profusion of watercress and fragrant mint. God surely created the spring with an abundance of love. It is protected on the east and west sides by steep hills dotted with oak, hickory, locust, and walnut trees. It is my favorite place to pray.

The spring was probably used by my grandparents for Cherokee medicine that required "going to the water." As part of a complex set of medicinal practices, it was said that dipping into water seven times during the fall when leaves fell into the water promoted healing. When I returned home, one of the first things I did was bathe in the ice-cold spring that held so many memories of my childhood.

Since we could not stay on the family land, Felicia, Gina, and I set up camp at Cherokee Landing near the site of the old Caney Creek, which now lay at the bottom of Lake Tenkiller, an artificial lake. From my childhood I could remember the time when Cherokee families camped on the banks of Caney Creek for days and cooked freshly caught fish in cast-iron skillets over an open fire.

Camping at Cherokee Landing was the best way to make the gradual transition from San Francisco to Stilwell. It was one of the rare times in my life when I had a great sense of freedom. We had no sense of urgency and few material possessions. Each day, we read or swam.

At night we built a fire and listened to music on a portable radio, talked, played Scrabble by the light of a Coleman lantern, or just watched the stars. We learned to tell time by the position of the Sun and the Moon. We delighted in sudden summer storms, and we eagerly awaited the end of each day when the Sun put on a spectacular show before we settled in for the night.

It was my intent to build a home on our family land. One day I went into the Adair County Courthouse to check on a land question. As I walked across the courthouse lawn, I overheard an elder Cherokee man say to another, "That's John Mankiller's granddaughter." The anonymity of San Francisco was gone forever. I was home.

Shortly thereafter, I encountered one of my many cousins, Maude Wolfe, a weathered, attractive Cherokee grandmother who in some inexplicable way reminded me of my father. I remembered her from his funeral four years earlier. Maude invited us to a Stomp Dance at the Flint Rock Ceremonial Grounds, presided over by her husband, Jim Wolfe, chief of the Four Mother Society. The Four Mother Society started as a religious and social movement in the late 1890s to oppose individual allotment of commonly held tribal lands. My daughters, Felicia and Gina, and I accepted an invitation to become members of the society.

It was late afternoon when we arrived at the grounds. There were four or five elder men sitting in lawn chairs watching a spirited game of stickball, and about a dozen other people were preparing a meal on a woodstove. Stickball is similar in some ways to the Haudenosaunee game of lacrosse. Though there are many stories about the origin and purpose of this game, I was told that rival Cherokee settlements once played stickball to settle disputes as an alternative to conflict.

Stickball was played in conjunction with ballplayers' dances and other ceremonies. On this day, the men were playing against the women, and Maude was one of the players. The men each carried a pair of stickball sticks, and the women used their hands. The object was to catch the small, round ball and throw it at an object on the top of a

ceremony

very tall pole. Those who successfully hit the object won points. That day the women won.

After the game, the women teased the men about their loss as everyone gathered for a supper of chicken and dumplings; brown beans; fish; large fluffy biscuits freshly cooked on the woodstove; bean bread; casseroles; homegrown cucumbers, onions, and tomatoes; and other fresh vegetables. Later there would be strong coffee, fruit pies, cobblers, and cakes. After the meal, Jim Wolfe and some of the other elders went back to their lawn chairs, which faced east toward the Stomp Dance grounds. They smoked, chewed tobacco, and only occasionally spoke.

After nightfall, people began to slowly drift toward the Stomp Dance grounds. Soon the dance would begin. In the past, there was a ceremony in which the medicine man prepared a central fire after dancing all night, and in the morning every person in the village took a new fire home from this specially prepared central fire. Putting out home fires then relighting them from the central fire was an important symbol of community and shared relationships. Elements of that traditional Cherokee ceremony were symbolized by the fire and rituals at Flint Rock Ceremonial Grounds.

At the appropriate time, Jim Wolfe walked onto the grounds, stood near the fire, and spoke to the people in Cherokee, as Cherokee spiritual leaders have done since time immemorial. When he finished speaking, he signaled to a designated person to begin the dances. I listened to the call and response of the songs, watched the dancers, and was soon drawn to the circle. From the moment I stepped into that circle of dancers, I felt embraced by the warmth of the fire and the rhythmic sound of the stones within the terrapin shells worn by the women. The division between the past and present dissolved. I felt whole again for the first time since my childhood.

Later, I learned that Cherokee people had always participated in similar seasonal dances to commemorate new corn, harvest time, and other events in the natural cycle of life. During these ceremonies, there was always a central fire. Though there was no sermon or written or oral dogma, the experience was palpably spiritual. Spirituality was not a separate, segmented part of life. It was life.

Soon after that night, Jim's daughter, Dorothy Wolfe, invited us to stay in an old house on her property, directly behind the Stomp Dance grounds. Seasoned campers by then, we were unfazed by the house's lack of indoor plumbing or other amenities. We were part of a community where Cherokee was spoken, traditional medicine was a part of everyday life, people talked about and tried to interpret dreams, and Cherokee knowledge was preserved in stories. We felt like the wealthiest people in the world.

Spiritual practices and religious beliefs among tradition-oriented Cherokee people differ greatly. Most are Christian and some follow traditional Cherokee ways, but outwardly there is little difference in the way tradition-oriented and Christian Cherokee people conduct their affairs, live their lives, and participate in the community. Though Charlie and I are involved in traditional Cherokee activities and ceremonies, we regularly attend Salem Church, whose parishioners are predominately Cherokee. The services and singing are frequently conducted in the Cherokee language. The church was one of the earliest members of the Cherokee Baptist Association, which some people credit with helping to preserve the Cherokee language through using it continually. Even those who are not Christian or literate in the Cherokee language greatly treasure the hymnals and Bibles written in Cherokee.

At least among some traditional leaders, the Bible is viewed as a collection of sacred stories from the people of the Middle East, which makes it more accessible. Sarah James says, "When Christianity was introduced to our people, they embraced it. They saw little difference between true Christian beliefs and our own traditional beliefs." Indeed, one of the most gifted Muscogee Creek traditional leaders who regularly participated in Flint Rock activities and ceremonies was a respected Baptist preacher. He and his group told stories

ceremony

about staying out all night at a Creek or Cherokee Stomp Dance and attending Sunday morning church services smelling of smoke from the central fire.

Certainly there are some Cherokee preachers who actively oppose the continuation of Cherokee traditional ceremonies and lifeways but others are tolerant of spiritual differences. When we first returned to Oklahoma and visited the ceremonial grounds of Stokes Smith, we often met Cherokee preachers there. Whatever their personal religious beliefs, there was mutual respect about their respective spiritual practices. They were all Cherokee people of faith.

As we adjusted to living close to the Wolfe Stomp Dance grounds and among many members of the Wolfe family, we slowly established a relationship with the land and came to appreciate the generosity of the natural world. It sustained us. We went fishing with the extended Wolfe family where we camped by the creek. The children were allowed the freedom to play, nap, or swim all day while the adults either fished or cleaned and cooked the fresh fish. We learned to make gravy out of wild grapes that my daughters picked from vines entangled in tree limbs. I would park my station wagon near a promising tree, and Felicia and Gina climbed on top of the car to reach the vines. The harder it was to gather the grapes, the better they tasted. Toward fall, we picked apples and gathered hickory nuts and walnuts. Every time I pass a certain hickory tree near Tahlequah, I remember the windy fall day when Maude Wolfe and I stopped there to gather nuts. She didn't have a sack or a bucket, so she gathered them into the skirt of her dress. Though she was generous, she carefully guarded the locations of the places where she gathered mushrooms, wild onions, or berries.

In 1978, when I was involved in a head-on collision with my friend, Sherrye Morris, Jim Wolfe came with medicine to help me heal. It is because of him that I am able to walk today. Sherrye was killed instantly and I came so close to dying that I experienced the seductive beckoning of death and an overpowering sense of complete, total well-being. I learned a lot during that terrible time. Brushing up against death matured me and absolutely convinced me that there is a spiritual world where unconditional love abounds.

Jim Wolfe told us stories about playing hide-and-go-seek with his grandfather, who could appear suddenly, seemingly out of nowhere, or quickly disappear. He said that the gift of changing or disappearing had been lost in his grandfather's time. Years later, when Jim Wolfe passed away, a single eagle flew in a circle above his burial site. Some said the eagle came to escort his spirit on its journey to the Creator's land. Others said it was just a good sign. By that time, I had come to understand that everything did not have to be explained. I simply acknowledged the fact that the eagle had come, and that it was good.

The Gathering
Rosalie Little Thunder

When I am in ceremony and smell the burning cedar, I remember the low voices of my grandfathers as they sang the ceremonial songs. I was privileged to hear these songs during a period when Lakota spirituality was underground, and I served as the lookout for the Catholic priest. When the Catholic priest discovered my existence, I was placed in boarding school. Although I can still recite Latin prayers and could probably sing the Latin high mass (if my life depended on it), I never forgot my father's words, "You can pray just about anywhere, and how you live is praying. Yup!" After many years of being despiritualized, as many of us were, I began practicing the traditional rituals, which was a slow and uphill recovery process. I still grieve for relatives that were despiritualized and now call our traditional rituals "witchcraft."

ceremony

Gail Small

In our language, Cheyenne means "beautiful people." There is a spiritual element to everything we do. Spirituality is the essence of Cheyenne people. Environment, culture, religion, and life are very much interrelated in the tribal way of life. Indeed, they are often one and the same. Water, for example, is the lifeblood of the people. I recall taking a draft tribal water code for public input into the five villages on my reservation when I was a tribal sociologist. Protection of the water spirits was a major concern throughout the reservation. And the water spirits were varied, depending on whether the water source was a river, lake, or spring. I reported back to the attorneys, and they laughed at my findings. However, it was no laughing matter when an elderly Cheyenne with a rifle kept the ARCO drilling team from crossing his water spring. "Today is a good day to die," he said as he held his own hunting rifle before him. I defended him in tribal court the next morning, and I cried with him when he told me how the water spirits sometimes came out and danced in his spring.

There is a profound spiritual dimension to our natural environment, and without it, the war would not be worth fighting. One of our leaders, Sweet Medicine, gave us four arrows and knowledge on how to live. Growing up with the land, one learns how everything is related. We look forward to the seasons and know what is coming into harvest or blooming, and we know and appreciate the beauty of the land.

Some white people look to us for help in their struggle with loss of identity, spirituality, and a sense of security. Unfortunately, we can't give that to them. They need to find it within themselves and their own cultures. When they try to appropriate tribal cultures, they have a negative impact on our culture and alienate themselves even more from their own ability to be centered.

Ella Mulford

As a Navajo, I was taught that all aspects of life are sacred. I was brought up with the concept of a higher authority. So, my traditional upbringing involved a lot of prayers and ceremonies. I don't know how to separate my spirituality from who I am. What I mean by this is that I go through life knowing there is a Creator who is all knowing, all good, and a protector. I can't imagine not having this knowing. Spirituality has helped indigenous people survive, and it gives us hope that we will see the next day's light. There was a period in my life when I abandoned my spiritual practice and had to find my way back. From my elders and my son Shawn, I came to understand that there was a process for achieving peace, which I believe is the purpose of spirituality. This process involves having a sense of identity, belonging, responsibility, and eventually a sense of peace. From our family and clanspeople we get our sense of identity. Once you know who you are and where you come from, you gain a sense of belonging. Your sense of belonging brings you to your sense of responsibility, and when you have taken care of that, your sense of peace.

Rosalie Little Thunder

We hold buffalo sacred and for good reason. They were the center of our existence; we depended upon them in extremely harsh conditions for survival. I can only compare their significance to the God of today: money.

The buffalo's greatest teaching was to show us how to live in balance with nature. Because we depended so much upon them for survival, we followed them in their migration path, never staying in one place long enough to destroy. The buffalo has great lessons on contributing to the health of the ecosystem: turning up the earth with its sharp hooves, fertilizing it, carrying seeds, and in its interdependencies with other species. We use the term Ikce Wicasa *to identify ourselves, meaning "common human," equal to all living things. This concept may escape the comprehension of those who have been*

ceremony

conditioned in the hierarchy that the human is above all. (And in what boat did we paddle to such arrogance?!)

Our spirituality is shaped around our relationships with all that is; our relationship of equality with the natural world, all living things, with each other, within ourselves, and with the Creator. And because the buffalo played such a significant role in survival, is it any wonder that they're held in such spiritual reverence?

The pipe and its moral teachings were brought to us by the White Buffalo Calf Woman. Most religions have a parallel figure that brought moral teachings to the people. The Christians have Moses. We believe in the White Buffalo Calf Woman just as deeply as Christians (many of my relatives) believe in Jesus Christ. Capitalists have Santa Claus.

In our own dependence upon the buffalo for sustenance, the killing was with proper ceremony, asking for forgiveness of the Creator and asking for the buffalo's surrender. There is also prayer for the release of the spirit so that it may live again. These rituals provided the necessary checks and balances against reckless and unnecessary killing.

Let me ask you this: what do you hold as sacred? And can you even imagine what you hold sacred being destroyed, being killed?

LaDonna Harris

I was raised among prayerful, spiritual people. People who have a strong sense of kinship, affection, and responsibility to one another. One of the things I respect about Comanche spirituality is there is no hierarchy or rigid structure. There are common beliefs, including that of a Creator, but each individual finds his or her own way to that place. My grandfather took me and my grandmother to church, and he would sit outside because he did not accept church teachings. He would sit outside and wait for us. That evening he would be singing peyote songs. He was a powerful man who could cure certain kinds of illnesses with his Indian medicine.

My grandfather was very wise. When I asked him if it bothered him that the church preached against the Native American Church and peyote, he

every day is a good day

said no one should try to take away anyone else's religious beliefs. He said it would be hurtful to everyone involved to try to take away the religious beliefs of others.

Some of the missionaries would come and preach in a way that was designed to make us question our identity. The message was that if we gave up music, dance, and our identity and then went to church, they might accept us. But they never accepted us.

Linda Aranaydo

Spirituality is where I always go for rest and renewal, where I go for healing. I can't imagine life without it. When I am out of balance, one sacred breath can bring me back into a good relationship with the world. Spirituality is not exclusive, and I don't have a label for it. It could be Catholic, Baptist, Buddhist, or Indian medicine—all of which are part of my upbringing and life experience. I feel comfortable going to any place where people go to pray, where people are meditating, where they are going inside themselves to be quiet for a while and just listen to life, or where they are being together to comfort one another in a sacred way. I've had to wrestle with the concept of Christianity and what churches and religions did to our people, but then Christ's messages are not violent. I finally made peace with all that. When my family comes back to Oklahoma for the Green Corn Ceremony at Hillubee Stomp Dance grounds, we take medicine together. The men sing, the women shake shells, and we dance in a spiral close to the fire. We let go of all negative things, get well together, and get into a good relationship with the world.

Octaviana Valenzuela Trujillo

Spirituality has sustained indigenous peoples since time immemorial. With the incursions into and eventual takeover of our traditional homelands by foreign interlopers, it has been the key to our very survival as a people. Just as it is our spirituality that defines us and our worldview as being a

ceremony

member of a specific indigenous group, it is also that spirituality that inter-
connects us as indigenous peoples across cultures throughout the world.

Spirituality has defined my sense of death and dying. My son,
Bopsy, gave me many lessons about life and life after death. He was
diagnosed with leukemia when he was five years old. It was in remission for
a year. He died when he was seven. He was my only child. Bopsy touched
many lives. When he died, all the church leaders came to honor him. We
had the Yaqui maestro, lay priest, Catholic, Pentecostal, and Presbyterian, all
wanting to participate in the funeral arrangements. They all knew my son.

During the time he was ill, I was approached by a mother of a child
who had died the year before from the same illness. She told me about a
group of individuals wanting to grant a special wish to terminally ill children.
Thus, Bopsy became the first child to receive his wish from the Make-A-
Wish Foundation, which recently celebrated its twenty-fifth anniversary.
Bopsy also became the first honorary fireman for the City of Phoenix.
Fireman Bill, who is retiring this year, gave an interview to the Arizona
Republic recently and named Bopsy as the person having the most impact
on his life.

Our elders still speak about the influence Bopsy had with all the
religious ceremonial leaders in our community. His understanding of death and
the afterlife gave me a new spiritual outlook. He accepted death as his fate at
a young age and gave me the strength to continue on this long journey, one
that I suspect he had made many times before the dying I came to witness.
There are many watershed experiences I have had with Bopsy that are
inexplicable yet knowable. His strong identity and his ability to impart his
spiritual fortitude to others from different cultures were remarkable.

Audrey Shenandoah

Our Onondaga traditional ways teach us that our ceremonies
originate from the Creator's land and that we have had them since the
beginning of time. Attaining peace of mind is paramount in all our ceremonies. We don't know how long our people lived in a ceremonial way before

every day is a good day

they began growing away from it. Their minds became polluted and finally, they were fighting and even killing each other. And that is when the Peace Maker came among us and the Great Law of Peace was established. The Great Law of Peace reinforced our traditional beliefs that being of good mind will bring about peace, and the longhouses were constructed and the ground council system of chiefs was established.

The Peace Maker brought a message of unity and peace to the people. He looked for the most powerfully evil man that everyone feared and took his message of goodness and peace to this man. The evil man enjoyed making everyone fearful of him and was reluctant to follow the good message of the Peace Maker. But the power of the message of peace overcame him and as he began to understand, he was changed. We are told that even his physical appearance changed as that evil slowly began to leave his mind. First, it left the mind, and then the body, until he was totally accepting of the message of peace. This is how powerful the message of peace can be. If people anywhere in the world would allow themselves to absorb a message of peace, it would change them in a powerful way. I was reading an editorial that states Arafat doesn't want peace in the Middle East; he wants Israel. If that editorial is true, he cannot move forward until he accepts peace.

After the Peace Maker came, the ceremonies and the thanksgiving continued until the white man came across the water. And once again pollution of the mind set in, the new ways of Europeans became very fascinating, and our people were pulling away from our old ways. Alcohol also altered the minds of our people. In our language, they call alcohol "mind twister" or "mind change." With all these new things coming at us, bombarding our way of life, the ceremonies continue and they give us peace of mind and a way to conduct ourselves.

We hold burial ceremonies in the longhouse. The burial has the same status as the Great Feather Dance. Our burial ceremony teaches everyone, including children, that death is the place we all have to pass through. We are told that each time a spirit leaves this Earth, a rattle and a song come down from the Creator's land. And so when a person passes away, we are with them. We do for them while they are still here on Earth and then when

ceremony

we take them and put them into the ground, that is as far as we can go with them. Then it is up to the Creator. In some longhouses, the Faith Keepers throw dirt into the place of burial, and then each person uses a shovel or just picks up a handful of dirt to throw in. We do what we can to help them pace their steps to meet the Creator.

Beatrice Medicine

Various Christian groups divided up the reservations. My father was a Catholic, and my sister Grace is a strong Catholic. The Delorias were Episcopalian. I was raised as a Catholic, but I believe in the Lakota religion. There are similarities in all religions—kindness, respect for the individual, a belief in spiritual power.

In the Sun Dance when the men pierce their chests, it isn't for themselves. It is for the welfare of the group. Women have a different role in the Sun Dance. They instruct the girls and then they dance with the pipe. There is also the sweat lodge where you can resolve a lot of things, obtain information and advice, and talk over whatever is bothering you without fear that it will be shared with others. Whatever is said in the sweat lodge stays there.

We all need a belief system. Christianity really disrupted the kinship unit. In the 1930s we weren't even allowed to go to some of the traditional funerals. Now, our people no longer go to the Christian churches, and they don't know their own Native belief systems. In a sense they are in spiritual limbo.

Joy Harjo

I just returned from the Green Corn Ceremony from my grounds, the Tallahassee Wvkokaye Grounds. The ceremony is about renewal, many levels of renewal. When I travel back to the grounds each summer I am traveling back to the heart of who I am and what I am in this world. This is about sovereignty. It is about spirituality, culture, everything that it takes to *maintain a human life with dignity in these times.*

I believe love is the strongest force in the world. It is the word and the concept I substitute for God. The word God in the English language is so tied up with the Euro-Christian tradition; I view God as a judgmental old white man without a sense of humor, presiding over heaven and hell. Heaven and hell are right here, inside of us, inside this world we occupy with each other. Recently, the Dalai Lama said he didn't believe in religion, he believed in love. In the Muscogee language, vnokeckv translates as "an overriding compassion" and is the root of Muscogee philosophy.

Jaune Quick-to-See Smith

I grew up understanding that the Sacred is the land, the sky, the water, and everything that goes with all of nature. The Sacred isn't housed in a building or worn around your neck or something in the sky. The Sacred is the here and now we reside in, all breathing the same air, all imbibing the same water and made of the same earth with "the life force" flowing through all living things. That mystical unknown is called by many names the world over, but is the same mystery. I call it Indian science because I think it has the most practical reality of any religion I know. By observation anyone can see the process for themselves, but the mystery of "the force" as the Star Wars *films call it, will never be understood—it will always be the Great Mystery or what we Salish call* Amotken.

European Christian value systems left their practical tribal knowledge behind and opted for a mythical world completely severed from nature and reality, with no respect involved. Genesis insists that humankind is in control of nature. I would like to see the day when humans can control a hurricane or the orbit of the Earth or its placement in the universe.

We, Indian people, have the only nature-based religion that is indigenous to the Americas. Our taboos, mores, social constructs, and teaching stories all come from the indigenous areas we originally lived in. The plants, animals, climate, and terrain were the outdoor classrooms that formed our worldview. The indigenous areas not only supplied our food and shelter, but they also

ceremony

determined our clothing, architecture, ceremonies, and life patterns. A brick sky-scraper in a city offers no such information except perhaps some information about the fleeting social standing of the occupants or how much they spend on food and clothing.

If humankind wrapped themselves around this notion of the Sacred, there would be more respect for the basic necessities we need in order to live, such as food, air, and water needed to secure a future for our progeny. Traditionally, we Native people are closer to Buddhists than we are to Christians and their hierarchical notion of life. Buddhists call life "the great net" and our place in it is only a tiny knot, the same status as all other living things and yes, including the insects. The Suyapis are busy getting ahead and putting things into categorical boxes, stripping them of their larger meaning and connectedness in order to plunder and pillage.

Traditional religion is powerful. Ten years ago, my cousin Gerald Slater, founder of our Salish Kootenai College, was told by Western doctors that he had very little time to live with his multiple myeloma, and there was nothing they could do for the pain in his ankles. The pain was so bad he could barely stand in the mornings. In desperation he turned to his brother-in-law, Conrad LaFromboise, a Blackfeet medicine man, though Gerald was a religious skeptic. After spending one day with Conrad and medicine people George and Millie Kicking Woman and G. G. Kipp, my cousin Gerald stood for the first time in months without pain.

We began ten years of steady attendance at the Okan (medicine lodge) ceremonies, which are summer encampments about renewal and giving thanks. Gerald also made the three-hour journey from Flathead to Blackfeet [Montana] for the Bundle Ceremonies through the spring and summer months. The traditional medicine bundles are closed for the winter after the ponds freeze over. I give credit to the power of the medicine for the extended years of Gerald's life. I also credit the medicine lodge for my son's vow that he would never drink alcohol again.

In quiet moments of my life, the Okan floods into my being with the flash of sudden memory. Sometimes at 3:00 in the morning I'll awake and recall the sound of the holy people drumming on an ancient painted

rawhide in the middle of the night. Or maybe I will look out a plane
window at 29,000 feet, and the plane's vibration reminds me of the stormy
wind hitting my tipi causing the ground to vibrate under my sleeping bag.
Sometimes I imagine how it feels to be touched when having my face painted
to receive a blessing from a holy person. Or I hear the dry rattle of the cot-
tonwood branches moving in time to the drum. Or the collective uhmmm
sound ending in a group chest thump as we all share in someone's good
luck coup story. The emphasis is on the collective, for no one medicine person
could emit the power that the participating collective puts forth. In each
case including waking in the morning, I am thankful. Thankful for my life,
health, my children and five grandchildren, my friends, my tribe, the holy
people, the Okan, and for the Sacred. Our traditional religion fills me up,
gives me strength, protection, and sustains me.

Angela Gonzales

Spirituality is a very private matter. It is part of who I am and what
I do. When I write, there is a prayer that goes into it. I hear people talking
about how they wake up in the morning and set aside twenty minutes a day
to meditate. When I wake up in the morning, I usually say a prayer without
a lot of fanfare. I don't go out on the balcony, arms outstretched. In our way,
it's very private, very personal. When I sit down for a meal, it's the same
thing. It's not something that I need to demonstrate. I am very aware of the
fact that there is a performative aspect of spirituality that many non-Indians
expect. They want to be able to see spirituality, to touch it. They ask, "Where
is your medicine bag? Where are all the things that symbolize your spirituality?" There is this kind of essential Indian list, everything from being an
enrolled member to wearing ethnic ornamentation. I feel just as comfortable
in my sense of being Hopi, dressed in street clothing. I don't feel the need to
wear it.

ceremony

Mary and Carrie Dann

We are different. When a Western Shoshone is allowed into this world as a child, the child is welcomed and blessed. Usually the aunt on the mother's side will bathe the child and ask one of the spiritual helpers to guide them through their lifetime. Our spiritual upbringing is critical. Our language, our beliefs, and the way we were raised shaped us. Indigenous worship includes every living thing. That is the way we worship. Our season of ceremonies is about life. We pray for all life: spirit life, human life, animal life, insect life. All life is included in seasonal ceremonies. I don't think other religions have anything similar to that. Maybe other indigenous religions do, but Christianity does not include all life. Those churches don't seem to show respect toward the Western Shoshone or other indigenous people. Many white people have no respect. They don't respect anything unless they're going to make money off of it. We have got to teach them respect for life, all life. They don't respect the other life out there, the animal life. They just take from them. The only time they think about animals is to hunt them for sport or something like that. Animals are part of the Creation, part of us. The elk are as important as we are, and so are the little bugs. They are part of the balance. Why are they out there? The elk and the little bugs? I often wonder why humans are here.

Sarah James

I believe the Creator has always been in my life, and now I believe in Christianity. The true Christianity is so close to how we believe and how we lived before contact. When Christianity came to us in our area, we were receptive to it because we already believed in that way of life. Later on, we found out that some of those who taught Christianity to us did not really live a Christian life.

Spirituality has played a great role in my life. It makes me committed to do more for the Earth. Without spirituality, one can't help oneself, others, or the Earth. I have seen the need to save the Earth, not only for me and for my people, but for the world. I grew up very close to the Earth, to the land, taking care of the land with my parents. We survived based on needs, not on greed. I received a good natural education that taught me how to ration things and survive on very little. I learned to respect the land. As I have traveled all over the world, I have heard indigenous people in many places say the Creator has asked us to be stewards of the land.

Joanne Shenandoah

Christianity, at least the organized part, played an important role in my life when I was a child. I was a member of a Protestant church, but at the same time I took part in the traditional longhouse rituals. As I grew older, I began to see how Christianity had altered our way of life and had divided our people. The missionaries might have been completely unaware of the consequences of their actions, as they believed their mission was inspired by God and sanctioned by the state. At the age of eighteen, I realized I could not function in a discipline that branded children as possessed by evil spirits until baptized, that taught us the world is full of evil and that women are secondary to men. I realized my own culture had more to offer me as a human being and as a woman. I learned that our Earth and all its elements are living entities to be celebrated and honored.

In our ways, we are taught not to fear aging, death, or what the next life holds. Life is considered a circle. There is so much to be thankful for and to relish in this life. Every morning I get up, burn some candles, maybe some sage, and listen to music. I love music. It lifts my spirits. From a young age, we are taught that we are given special gifts and we are supposed to use those gifts in an appropriate way and to share with others in a good way. For me, it is music. I hope my music helps bring people to a place of solitude and peace.

Future generations of children need to know the joy and sense of community we feel when we are all together, eating, praying, singing. We all understand our place in the community, where we are safe. We carry with us a story of the cornhusk doll. This story is about a young woman who loses her face because she thought she was better than everyone else. Our natural gifts are given to us to use in a good and positive way. It is said that if we use our Creator-given talents, the planet will then be a better place to live.

There is nothing more beautiful in life than experiencing ceremonies with my loved ones. No matter what is going on in our lives, we remain strong because we come from such a powerfully sound place. When we step inside the longhouse, we leave outside the door any angry feelings or other things we disagree on and come together with a good mind to celebrate this beautiful gift of life together. In order to have a good mind and walk the Earth in a comfortable way, and into the Creator's land, one has to learn to let go and to forgive.

Lurline Wailana McGregor

A truly spiritual person projects love and respect for all things and does not harbor negative thoughts or feelings. I constantly strive to act with love and compassion, and to live a life that is meaningful for me as a Native Hawaiian. Spiritual practices are an important part of continuing the culture. I don't think of Akua, or the Creator, as a Christian God. I think that can be very confusing and limiting, especially since religions can be so political and economically driven, and have often been a source of divisiveness and war instead of unity. In the Hawaiian realm, there is a supreme God, but there are also many lesser deities that must also be acknowledged and fed. Yet it is through love that we carry out these practices, rather than through fear of punishment. We will make offerings to Pele when we approach the volcanoes; we acknowledge Kanaloa when we go to the sea; and we ask permission and give thanks when we gather materials from the 'aina (land) to fulfill our needs. Ritual is very important. It requires a great deal of discipline, but when we carry out these traditions with love and respect we grow spiritually and begin to understand the meaning and purpose of all things.

Florence Soap

I started going to church when I was about thirteen years old. We went to church a lot. We used trails in the woods to walk to and from church. At night we would use a lantern to light the trail. As Christians we are taught to love everybody because God wants us to love each other. When I was well, I would go to the hospital and sit with people or cook for people. God taught me that. We also went to Cherokee Stomp Dances, and we used Cherokee traditional medicine. My mother-in-law, Molly Soap, taught me a lot about medicine. I used to help her gather medicine in the woods. She was a good woman and a good healer who lived to be more than 110 years of age. She served as a midwife for most of my children.

She could treat many illnesses. But there are diseases now that are new to our people. Back then there was very little arthritis or diabetes. To treat people she used fire and water, and she would say the right words in Cherokee. Being able to heal is a gift from God. Some people claim they are healers, but they just want money. You can tell a good medicine person if you use the medicine and it helps you, heals you. If it doesn't work, then the person is not a good medicine man or woman. You have to be able to speak Cherokee to be a Cherokee medicine person. How can you say the right Cherokee words if you can't speak Cherokee? God is the one that gives healers the ability to help people.

Debra LaFountaine

I grew up in a family of eleven children with an abusive, alcoholic father. My mother was totally dependent on my father, who was not able to be there for her. As the oldest daughter, it was expected that I would take care of my brothers and sisters and serve as a mother and friend to my mother as well. My siblings and I spent time in orphanages and foster homes while my parents were trying to get things figured out. Needless to say, this had a great impact on the direction my life would take, and these experiences would dictate my worldview for a very long time. From my childhood experiences I

ceremony

had the idea that a woman was relatively powerless. I promised myself that I would not be powerless. I decided to make sure I would not be dependent on anyone for anything.

My life changed dramatically one night when I was thirty-four years old. I was feeling exhausted and empty inside, and I could not sleep even though I had worked for eleven hours at my job that day. I went out to sit on my front-porch swing for a while. Sitting there alone, tired and sleepy, it occurred to me that I had achieved a level of success in one area of my life but I was a total failure in another. I had created a life devoid of meaningful personal relationships. I was in the middle of a divorce from a good man. Friends and family had stopped calling because I was always too busy to see them. Work was a priority for me. I was determined to be successful and I had no time to nurture relationships. My definition of success was always the next promotion, degree, or material acquisition. If I achieved a level of professional success, I just knew somehow I would be happy.

Sitting on my porch swing that night, I began to talk to the Creator even though I wasn't even sure if I believed in the Creator. I asked him if this was all there is to life. I couldn't connect with any kind of purpose in my life. I asked the Creator to lead me to a direction with meaning. I wanted to serve a greater purpose than living just for myself. I decided the Creator had something in mind for my life, and I just needed to make myself open and available to it. The very next day I gave notice that I was quitting my job. After spending several months trying to figure out what I might do that had some meaning and purpose, I finally prayed for some direction. Through a set of relatively strange circumstances, I heard about a job opening at the Native American Rights Fund, a nonprofit legal advocacy organization. One of the questions they asked stopped me in my tracks: "What have you done for your people?" That single question made me understand the purpose of my life. For the first time in my life I understood that I was accountable for helping the people. Eventually I was led to the place where I could work and be of service to the people. Once I began to work for the people, I spent a great deal of time with elders who seemed like the Creator's guides sent to teach me about life. Although I can't say I have perfect faith, I can say I see *more of life's journey than I ever thought possible. I no longer pay attention to the things that distracted me from life: what I have or don't have, how I look, what others think about me. I have a path and a purpose. It is an inner focus. Now I ask myself, "How am I conducting myself as I take this journey through life?"*

As I became more focused on the message of the elders, I learned that peace starts from within and works its way out. If one begins to heal oneself, to walk one's own path and understand one's purpose, the rest will follow. The elders help to lead me back to prayer and ceremony, and in this I have found some semblance of peace, which has allowed me to be thankful for all the difficulties and challenges and to accept my journey through life. Prayers and ceremony helped me to gain a different perspective on my life and see it all in a different light.

Through spirituality I gained a greater understanding of my parents. During her childhood, my mother attended Chemawa Indian Boarding School in Oregon. When she got with my father, she was very young and did not have good self-esteem. They had fourteen children together, three of whom died during childbirth. We ended up in foster homes because my mother was overwhelmed by having to deal with my father and take care of all of us. My parents loved each other in their own way, but my father didn't know how to be a good father and husband to my mother. He only knew what his alcoholic and abusive father had shown him.

My mother was a Catholic who did not believe in divorce, but after thirty-four years she did leave him. My father eventually became homeless. When my mother was close to death from terminal cancer, my siblings and I went home and took turns being with her. She was still angry with my father and said she would not forgive him even though we told her that if she forgave our father, she could let go. Then a few days before her death, she said God came to assure her that she was going to a really good place, and he told her to take care of business. She told my sister to go find my father. When my father went into my mother's room, he closed the door, and there was a lot of crying. Everything between them got taken care of. It was like God had finally come and said, "You have got to forgive him because I can't bring you

ceremony

over here with hatred in your heart." And so she did. Less than a year later, my father told my sister, "Your mom came to me, and she was so young and beautiful, and she wanted me to come over." Soon after that, they found him dead in his pickup.

It took me a long while to understand how to look at my past and see it for what it really was. It was perfection. This is what I believe to be true. All life is perfection. My mother and father were the best parents to me that they could possibly have been. I am who I am because of them. My strength comes from them, my desire to be of service comes from them, and they gave me what I needed in this life to help me walk my journey in a good way.

Faith Smith

Spirituality is with us all the time. We give thanks to the Creator because we are happy or able to take care of our family and grateful for having enough food to eat. We give thanks because we have friends that are important to us. We give thanks because our parents are well. Then we give thanks for the people who loved us and gave so much of themselves to help us, some of whom are not here anymore. Spirituality is a part of everything we do.

context is everything

Chapter Three

*The kinship unit is very powerful.
I want my descendants to have a strong
sense of who their ancestors were and to
understand who they are in the larger
Lakota cultural base. I want them to understand that they have a responsibility to be
a conduit for our culture. That is the only
hope we have of ensuring
the essence of our culture will continue,
even if it takes a diluted form.*
—Beatrice Medicine, Lakota

What do we mean by *indigenous culture* and *lifeways*, and why is it important that we maintain them? Some people describe cultural attributes as language, medicine, songs, ceremony, the land, and the community, and some simply define culture as lifeways. The response to the question of what constitutes culture will vary from community to community and individual to individual, though there is probably general agreement that living according to a certain set of values is one of the most important attributes of culture. Traditional indigenous values can be maintained whether one lives in an urban area or on tribal homelands.

Most non-Native Americans know little about the governments of indigenous people and even less about the values and lifeways of indigenous people. This lack of accurate information has produced a number of stereotypes, including that of the mystical child of nature—spiritual but incapable of higher thought—or the bloodthirsty savage who murdered and scalped innocent settlers. Whether indigenous people are romanticized or vilified, they are rarely viewed as whole human beings. After all these years of interaction with Euro-Americans, indigenous people still have no identity except that which has been created by stereotypes.

A significant number of people believe tribal people still live and dress as they did 300 years ago. During my tenure as principal chief of the Cherokee Nation, national news agencies requesting interviews sometimes asked if they could film a tribal dance or if I would wear traditional tribal clothing for the interview. I doubt they asked the president of the United States to dress like a pilgrim for an interview. More than one visitor to the Cherokee Nation capitol in Tahlequah, Oklahoma, has expressed disappointment when they see no tipis or tribal people dressed in buckskin. When these crestfallen tourists ask, "Where are all the Indians?" I sometimes place my tongue in my cheek and respond, quite truthfully, "They are probably at Wal-Mart."

For centuries outsiders have tried to explain the differences in worldview between indigenous people and the larger society by trying to analyze the ineffable spirit of tradition-oriented indigenous people. Most research has been conducted on the assumption that indigenous people process information the same way as Euro-Americans, but that cultural differences cause them to think about different things. Though considerable environmental and cultural differences are certainly a factor, I am convinced there is an entirely different way of processing information among tradition-oriented indigenous people that is more whole and complete, and considers the contradictions and unevenness of life. By and large, Euro-Americans tend to be more analytical, to categorize things, rely on formal logic, and avoid contradictions, while tradition-oriented Native Americans view things in a more interrelated way. Audrey Shenandoah says, "The way we describe it in our language—we are all connected. We don't describe the natural world as separate. We are part of the natural world, and the natural world is part of us. And we are all family. This way of thinking keeps us connected to the whole universe."

Though many non-Native Americans have learned very little about us, over time we have had to learn everything about them. We watch their films, read their literature, worship in their churches, and attend their schools. Every third-grade student in the United States is presented with the concept of Europeans discovering America as a "New World" with fertile soil, abundant gifts of nature, and glorious mountains and rivers. Only the most enlightened teachers will explain that this world certainly wasn't new to the millions of indigenous people who already lived here when Columbus arrived.

People in the United States fail to recognize how much they have been influenced by indigenous people. It is simply amazing that even after hundreds of years of living in our former villages, most Americans don't know much about the original people of this land. In his groundbreaking book, *Indian Givers: How the Indians of the Americas Transformed the World,* Dr. Jack Weatherford argues that America has yet to be discovered as he traces the birth of modern pharmacology to indigenous people and documents many other important but little-known contributions.

In the many dozens of national discussions and debates about the critical need to preserve the Amazonian rain forests and the Arctic National Wildlife Refuge, indigenous people are rarely even a consideration. There are very few references to the indigenous peoples who have lived with these lands for thousands of years and have a tremendous amount of knowledge to share.

The knowledge and culture of the world's indigenous people hold many potential gifts for the world. One of the most important challenges of our time is to figure out the best way to capture and maintain traditional knowledge systems. Whenever a traditional elder passes on, they take with them thousands of years of unique knowledge that had been passed down from generation to generation. This tribal knowledge and the stories give Native people a sense of identity, of belonging, of knowing their place in the world.

In the larger society around us, there is scant recognition of the importance of maintaining traditional indigenous knowledge. In some cases, our people remain objects of curiosity instead of people who have important knowledge to share. Rather than appreciate the ancient cultures of indigenous people in the United States, most governmental policies have been designed to assimilate indigenous people into the larger American culture. But what exactly is American culture? Even with the dramatically changing racial composition of the United States, a preoccupation with European culture remains. Most of the Americans who want to assimilate Native Americans are hard-pressed to define American culture. In the year 2000, one enthusiastic reporter described the finale of the voyeuristic television show *Survivor* as "the greatest cultural event since Armstrong landed on the Moon." Indeed, more than 40 million American people gathered in their homes and at "finale parties" to watch the concluding episode of this twelve-week television show in which sixteen contestants lived on a remote island with few rules, except to win $1 million by undermining each other. The last contestant to survive, a ruthless, scheming corporate planner, plotted against his colleagues to win the money. Similar so-called "reality" programs have been developed throughout the Western world. If this is what constitutes reality in American culture, it doesn't hold much appeal to the women at this gathering who struggle to remain genuine in a world where material wealth reigns supreme, many people are distant from the natural world, and kindness is perceived as weakness. LaDonna Harris says, "In the Comanche way, we don't accumulate things for ourselves, we accumulate them so we can do good for others. In the old way, our people redistributed their material wealth through giveaways and other methods. In contemporary times, we continue that tradition by giving away knowledge, ideas, information, and resources." Linda Aranaydo adds, "People think of value in terms of what they have accumulated. They think if one has the ability to accumulate wealth, they can be spared pain, suffering, or difficult times. And then people are disappointed because they keep buying and accumulating, and they're still in pain." Faith Smith continues, "Their economic system defines who is important and who is not. That is certainly one of the differences between us."

Many of the women at the gathering have long-term personal and professional partnerships with people who understand their issues and support their work. When they discuss the differences between white people and tradition-oriented indigenous people, they are not referring to racial or biological differences alone, but to a society of obsessively acquisitive people who have a disproportionate sense of entitlement based on their race. They are referring to people with a completely different way of thinking and living who have little appreciation for those with other values and lifeways. Gail Small speaks passionately about her frustration with white racism in the towns bordering her reservation, but she also speaks with great admiration and respect for a white lawyer who devoted many years, without compensation, to helping Northern Cheyenne get a high school on the reservation. At the office of the Dann sisters, young white women work alongside Western Shoshone people as full partners in a fight to protect Shoshone lands, and Sarah James speaks glowingly of the white supporters who have worked for years to help them protect the Arctic National Wildlife Refuge. Rosalie Little Thunder says, "There are basic differences between us and them, but it is not always race. I know some indigenous people who are wasteful, controlling, and thoughtless, and I know some light-skins that are thoughtful and careful. In a collective sense, though, indigenous peoples

context is everything

are equipped with genetic memories that demand some degree of loyalty and attention." Joy Harjo adds, "It is pure insanity to define people solely by the color of their skin." And there are many examples of outstanding white partners and supporters such as historian Angie Debo, who made a profound positive difference in the lives of Native people. While it is clear that biology is not the sole determinant of vast cultural differences, there is little question that significant cultural differences exist between tradition-oriented indigenous people and members of the larger society around them.

Wilma Mankiller

My early childhood in an isolated, predominately Cherokee community shaped the way I view the world. I learned a lot about community and reciprocity by observing how our extended family and neighbors depended on one another for support and survival. In those days, everyone helped one another, sometimes trading goods—eggs for milk or farm goods for store-bought goods. People were not as hurried as they are today, and visitors sometimes stayed well into the night or until the next day. While the adults played cards or talked, we children played games such as hide-and-go-seek, kick the can, or marbles. Occasionally we held a contest to see who could ring the most wall nails with the rubber rings from mason jars. We also made up new games. The natural world was our playground, and we used our imaginations to invent interesting things to do. During the day, we spent scant time in the small wood frame house built by my father—our work and play was mostly outside. Time was defined by the natural rhythms of the land. Even today some Cherokee elders describe events by the time when certain crops are ripe or foods are gathered, rather than by a calendar, and they can tell time by the Sun with great accuracy.

We had little access to the world outside our community.

every day is a good day

There was no paved road near our house. We had no indoor plumbing, electricity, or even a well. When we were not working, our family passed the time by playing board games, cards, or listening to stories. There were stories about owls as bearers of bad news and stories about outlaws such as Pretty Boy Floyd burying treasure nearby, arranging for it to be guarded by rattlesnakes. We heard stories about Cherokee Little People who could sometimes be heard speaking Cherokee or singing near freshwater springs and creeks. Most of the stories taught a valuable lesson about life.

Yet our childhood was not always an idyllic time of playing and games. Each morning we walked the three miles to Rocky Mountain School and then back again at the end of the day. And my family and everyone else in our community worked very hard. My sister Linda and I sometimes gathered water for drinking and household use from a freshwater spring about a quarter mile from our home. My older brothers and sisters cut wood, hauled water, helped wash an endless supply of clothing and dishes, and even contributed to the family income by earning money picking beans or strawberries or cutting wood for railroad ties. But it was my oldest brother, Louis Donald, who worked the hardest. He went with my father to Colorado, along with other Cherokee men, to cut broomcorn. The money he and my father earned bought clothes and shoes for my siblings and me for the winter.

While preparing logs to sell for railroad ties, my sister Frances severely cut her knee and had to be taken to Hastings Indian Hospital in Tahlequah. After her hospitalization, she stayed with relatives for some time. Not too long after that terrible accident, my father signed our family up for the Bureau of Indian Affairs Relocation Program, which promised a better life for our family. We had no idea what to expect when we gathered at the train depot in Stilwell, Oklahoma, in the fall of 1957 to prepare for the journey to San Francisco.

We didn't know how to prepare for or even think about our new life in San Francisco. The farthest we had been from home was

context is everything

about forty miles away to the Muskogee County Fair. It is a gross understatement to describe our relocation experience as culture shock. Checking into the old Keys Hotel in the Tenderloin District of San Francisco was like landing on Mars. The sights, smells, sounds, and feel of the place were dramatically different from anything we had ever known. The better life the Bureau of Indian Affairs promised us turned out to be a minimum-wage job for my father and Louis Donald and life in a tough urban housing project for our family. Like many other families relocated from their tribal homelands to the cities, we made connections with other Native people who had been relocated to San Francisco from reservations and tribal communities across the United States. Our social life centered on the old San Francisco Indian Center, where my father found a Cherokee-speaking family to converse with. That Indian center burned down not too long before the occupation of Alcatraz Island in 1969.

When the Alcatraz occupation occurred in November of 1969, I was a twenty-three-year-old housewife and mother of two young daughters. I had married Hector Hugo Olaya, an Ecuadorian college student, just before my eighteenth birthday. My husband had definite and fairly narrow ideas about the role of women. I was to be attractive, an excellent cook, a great household manager, and devote most of my energy and time to being his wife and the mother to our children. It is a role that some women relish but one that I could not fill, even though I tried. Sometimes I would look across the room at the father of my children and wish I could find a way to be the person he wanted me to be. It just was not possible. I wanted to be engaged in the world around me, to be involved in politics, civil rights, women's rights. San Francisco was an exciting place to be in the early 1970s. I wanted to be more active in the Native American community, not just as a volunteer. I wanted to learn more about the Cherokee world I had left more than a decade earlier. And I wanted to be part of a community again.

As I became increasingly active in the Pit River Tribe's land claim struggle, as well as the Bay Area Indian community, tensions rose in my relationship with my husband. It was difficult trying to balance all that. He had the only car and determined when and where we would go when we traveled out of the city. One simple act of independence changed all that. I secretly withdrew money from our joint savings account and bought my own car—a new candy apple–red Mazda.

I loved that car. With my daughters, Felicia and Gina, I visited the Rags and Ida Steele family on the Pomo Kashia Ranchero, where we were always warmly welcomed. It was such a joy to leave the Bay Area and travel less than one hundred miles to an indigenous world that welcomed and embraced us. While at Kashia, we stayed in the Steele family's small wood frame house, which was not unlike the home of my childhood. In warm months, Ida had a "cook place" in front of the house where she prepared thick tortillas on a grill over an open fire. She filled these tortillas with tiny surf fish and the fresh seaweed we had gathered in old and battered but still sturdy Pomo baskets. One of my fondest memories of that time is going to the ocean with a group of Pomo women to gather seaweed for the evening meal. Rags worked at a local winery, so we always had fine wine with our meals and plenty of it afterward as well. At night we often sat outside and the Steele family shared stories about Pomo history and culture. We loved Kashia. Felicia and Gina danced in the Kashia Round House where Pomo elder Essie Parrish presided, and we attended the Strawberry Festival, which always reminded me of my Oklahoma hometown of Stilwell, which also hosts an annual strawberry festival and claims to be the strawberry capital of the world.

We traveled to Pit River in Yurok Country and to central California to visit the Mono people. In 1974 Maxine Steele and I packed up the Mazda, gathered our children, and left for the Colville Reservation to attend a spiritual gathering following the Wounded Knee occupation. Maxine's brother Charley and my brother Richard had both been at the occupation in South Dakota. When we arrived at the camp, the first thing we noticed was the tight security. This was during the height of federal paranoia about the American Indian movement, especially for anyone who had participated in the Wounded Knee occupation. Strong young men wearing red armbands protected the camp from intruders, just as their ancestors had done so long ago.

Once inside the camp, many tents and campfires could be seen. We could hear Dakota-movement musician Floyd Red Crow Westerman singing and playing the guitar. There were meetings in some of the tents. I felt so honored to be invited to sit in on a couple of the meetings. I never said a word. I just listened. It was in those tents that I heard people, some quite elderly, speaking passionately about their willingness to fight to protect tribal lifeways and lands. I also made mental note of the decorum of the group, which was circumspect and respectful to one another. Leadership, as in historic Cherokee communities, was exerted by the power of persuasion, not by threat of force or coercion. We traveled to many other tribal communities and events all over the West Coast. By the time I finally traded the red Mazda to my brother for a buffalo robe, my marriage was over, and I knew I would soon be going home to Oklahoma.

My first job with the Cherokee Nation began in October of 1977. People did not quite know what to make of me. I cheerfully worked longer hours than most anyone, and I would do whatever it took to get something done. My secretary would often find me sitting on the floor of my office trying to collate a grant proposal while my colleagues were worrying about the state of their bouffant hairdos. By then I had an abiding belief that a distinct and vibrant Cherokee culture which should be more fully supported existed in some historic Cherokee communities.

Cherokee traditional identity is tied to both an individual and a collective determination to follow a good path, be responsible and loving, and help one another—or as some Cherokee traditionalists say, "Not let go of one another." The whole self-help concept of community development and the founding of the Cherokee Nation Community Development Department was based on the simple premise that when given the resources and opportunity, tradition-oriented Cherokee people will help each other and take on projects for the larger community good. Gadugi, or working collectively for the common good, is an abiding attribute of Cherokee culture.

The Gathering
Audrey Shenandoah

The main difference between our people and the world around us is our thankfulness and respect for the Earth, our environment, and the natural world. In our way, every day is a good day. We would never think of asking for a good day, what you would call a nice day in English. When it rains, people just accept it and go on. Our people know more about acceptance and contentment than our white brothers and sisters who seem to think they have to be deliriously happy all the time. They are looking for something that their world doesn't offer them. It makes them unhappy if things are not the way they think they should be. They spend a lot of time trying to find happiness rather than finding peace of mind. Our seasonal cycle of ceremonies are to bring peace of mind. Healing is left to the Creator.

The spiritual values are the key to our survival. It is very important to keep the ceremonies going and perpetuate the ways our elders handed down to us. This should be paramount in our minds and in our lives. Today we are having a hard time keeping our ceremonies going at the appropriate times because people have to work at a job in order to survive. There is no more subsistence from the land because the land base is so small. The hunting isn't that good. Our men and boys have to travel far up north for good hunting and fishing.

Some young people seem to think we are preoccupied with our tra-ditions and old ways. They say, "You've got to deal with reality. Deal with what's real." Well, what is more real than the Earth, the water, the wind, the plant life and the animal life? All of that is real. The other world is not reality at all. In that world there is an urgency to make lots of money and

context is everything

then stockpile it. They try to keep lots of money coming in so they can buy things they don't need. Everything is consumable and has to be replaced after it is used up. Everywhere on television and radio, we are continually given the message that everything is a commodity, even people. It is a mixed-up world if people believe that is reality.

Our white brothers and sisters are always praying for something. They have no grounding or anything to tell them that things are all right. They are always in need of making things better or needing more and thinking things should be better. I'm not trying to say that it's not good to try to make things better. In fact, one of our traditional laws teaches us we are supposed to make things as good as we can. It is illustrated all the way through our history that we are supposed to do our best at whatever we are doing, and this is accept-able to the Creator. We have a story about a time when the Faith Keepers asked some men to go out and get thirty deer for the ceremony. So they went through the proper ceremonies to prepare themselves and cleanse themselves so they would have a good mind to go looking for food for the people. They went out and tried their very best. When they came back they had twenty-eight deer and one small bear. They were not able to get thirty deer but they had done their best, and this was acceptable to the Creator.

When we meet, we put our minds together as one mind and give thanks for everything—the Earth, the medicine, the foods, the woodlands, the stars, Grandmother Moon, the winds, everything. We acknowledge their worth, acknowledge that we are equal with the woodland, the trees, the berries, the two-legged and the four-legged. We share the same air, space, and water. We all need the same things to live. Everything in the cycle is always giving. If one thing drops out of the cycle, then the rest would be out of balance and soon cease to exist. But if humans were to drop out of the cycle, the rest would go on and become healthy again.

Acknowledge is a very important word in our language. You say it every time you meet someone. You acknowledge them as a sign of respect. In our language, you are saying, "I am thankful you are well when we meet." And when we acknowledge all the rest of Creation, we are acknowledging their existence as equals to us. We are not the strongest of everything in life's cycle. Man thinks he is superior and dominant over everything, even moving the Earth or trees at his discretion, and that everything else in Creation is a commodity that he can use or make money on. And that is why the world is out of balance.

Beatrice Medicine

White people can't understand us or the strength and diversity of aboriginal people, and they don't even try. That's why there is such racism and misunderstanding. We have different attitudes toward one another. We honor each other. When they first encountered Native people, they tried to understand us because their very lives were dependent upon the relationships and trade for food and other items. But after they started obtaining the land, all they could think about is land as productive units. White people are more acquisitive and concerned with the individual, whereas our chiefs thought about everyone. They were warriors who also had to take care of the elderly, the children, widows, and children without parents.

My whole career has been oriented to teaching people the essence of what it means to be a Lakota person. The only hope we have of ensuring we maintain our culture is to start very early to teach children about the culture and the language and then tie the language in with attitudes and beliefs. The essence will still be there, even if it is in diluted form. My nephew has done a very good job of raising his children so they have a strong sense of who they are. They are trying to learn the Lakota language, and they practice our rituals. They dance in the Sun Dance.

We are reviving a beautiful girl's puberty ceremony where each girl has a mentor. The mentor is the female embodiment of the Lakota culture. And the boys go on a vision quest, and their mentor interprets the vision for them. The mentor also prepares him for adulthood and teaches him how to respect and treat women.

context is everything

Gail Small

At Northern Cheyenne we look at history quite differently. Our history is the premise of who we are and how we make our decisions today. The stories we have heard about the Sand Creek Massacre, especially the things they did to our grandmothers, are very powerful and personal. There are stories about American soldiers cutting off the breasts and vaginas of Cheyenne women, drying them out, and then using them as saddle ornaments. What we've gone through and what our ancestors have gone through is so real, it is like it happened yesterday. At our council meetings, when we have had disputes about how to fight the coal companies and figure out what direction we should go, elders help us stay focused when they get up in the council and tell inspirational stories. They tell stories of when we all walked to Northern Cheyenne from Oklahoma on the Cheyenne Trail of Tears. Sometimes they will tell the story of the Battle of Rosebud, where a young girl saved her brother. These elders would never give advice. They just tell the stories and sit down. It centers the people, grounds them, and gives them perspective. When elders try to settle disputes by telling stories, the white lawyers and government officials never really understand what is going on.

We have a lot of stories. These stories give us the strength and wisdom to make the right decisions. One important story is about the time when our people were starving and Head Chief and Young Mule took a white man's beef to feed our people. The United States Cavalry, which was camped at a fort in nearby Lame Deer, Montana, planned to take Head Chief and Young Mule as prisoners for taking a white man's beef to feed our starving people. Head Chief and Young Mule decided they would rather die as free people in battle than go to the white man's prison. They sent word to the cavalry that they would descend a certain hill and advised the cavalry to stand at the base of the hill. At the appointed time, Head Chief and Young Mule dressed up in their warrior clothing and went to the top of the hill. Almost immediately, the cavalry shot the elder man's horse out from under him. Head Chief got up and started down the hill dancing a beautiful war

every day is a good day

dance in full regalia. As he danced his way down the hill, Young Mule was charging down the hill on horseback. The cavalry repeatedly tried to shoot Head Chief and Young Mule, but each time they missed. When Head Chief had danced and Young Mule rode to a point near the bottom of the hill, they were both killed by the cavalry. The message of this story is that it is better to live free and to die free with dignity. The U.S. military and government tried to trivialize our heroic history by calling that hill "Squaw Hill." Cheyenne women and children organized ourselves and successfully changed the name so that it is no longer called Squaw Hill.

There is another story about the time when Franciscan nuns first arrived and built a mission. They had good intentions and really tried to understand the people. It was a time when the buffalo were being killed and our people were forced to learn how to live on a small area of land. The nuns helped the Cheyenne people grow different crops along the river. I have heard stories about how well the people liked those nuns. That is one of the few times in history when white people wanted to help without demonizing our people or wanting to take what we had. Unfortunately, when the priests came, they pushed aside the nuns and took over the mission.

It is the Creator Maheo's miracle that we still have this beautiful homeland. You can feel the spirits within our homeland. Many Cheyenne gave their lives for us to live in this beautiful North Country, and they guide us yet today. I believe in water spirits, all aspects of Cheyenne culture, because I have seen and felt their power. There is a reason for everything the Cheyenne believe.

My sister, Geri, president of our tribe, carries tremendous responsibility. Today she is at our most sacred mountain, Bear Butte, praying. She knows that she cannot do it alone, and her faith is strong. She goes to the mountain for strength and guidance, and she always comes home strong. As Cheyenne we have no choice but to continue the life of fighting for our tribe's homeland and culture—no matter the odds. Right now, our reservation is becoming like an island, surrounded by this country's energy Goliaths who want our coal, oil, and gas. They want to drain our groundwater just so they can obtain a little more methane coal-bed gas. We are up against tough odds

context is everything

in this methane fight. And there are always other battles to be fought. It is a very tough time for the Cheyenne.

The main difference between white people and Cheyenne people is how we view life. We view life here on Earth as a very short journey. We are not driven by the need to accumulate material things or by greed. In the American way of thinking, everything is very fractionated. Their life and their church are distinctly different. Whereas among the Cheyenne, everything is centered on the Creator. All human beings are like one small spoke in a big wheel of Creation. There is no hierarchy, and the Creator is at the center of the wheel.

We have fought so hard for our land. Our land is what we all coalesce around. We may disagree about all these other issues, but when it comes to the land, Cheyenne people rally together. I have a hard time envisioning a living culture without a land base, without our ancestors' land.

Faith Smith

There is a difference in values. Several years ago my son decided to join a traditional tribal society, which involves meetings and ceremonies during the initiation period. At the same time the ceremonies were being held, he was to be at the first meeting of a prestigious fellowship program. He made a conscious choice to miss the fellowship program meeting so he could participate in the ceremonies. To the larger society, his choice probably wouldn't make much sense. But to us, it was the right choice. He placed a higher value on the traditional ceremony than the fellowship.

When I was a child, I lived in the country with my grandparents on the reservation, and I attended a Bureau of Indian Affairs day school. Being at that school was like living in a box. When I went fishing with my grandfather or we went off in the woods or set his beaver traps, that was the time of the greatest freedom and comfort, knowing I was safe and everything was okay. My grandparents did not want us to speak Ojibway because they did not want us to be separate from the other students. They wanted us to figure out how to maneuver in the world. There was a lot of pressure on my *grandparents to send me off to be educated at a boarding school. What I learned from that experience is that there was someone on the outside that didn't place much value on my parents and grandparents, and thought I would be better off away from them.*

Another situation illustrates the continuing misunderstanding and racism we have to deal with. During a time of great financial difficulty, our college had to undergo an evaluation from the North Central Accreditation Association. What little money we had to pay for salaries we divided equally among all staff, whether they worked as a janitor or as the president, which was me. We all had families that had to eat. We all had to take care of sick kids and make car payments, and we were all giving of our time and were there for the same reason. This pay arrangement reflected our values and our obligations to one another, as well as our sense of community. The North Central people could not even remotely understand this concept and thought we should have just kept the top administrators. Their economic system defines who is important and who is not. That is certainly one of the differences.

Linda Aranaydo

How could anyone not just love the sound and tone of our language? The Muscogee Creek people get together to pray, sing, and feed the people. And that's done in the church and the Stomp Dance grounds. We come together as a community of faith, and some of that is faith in God and some of that is faith in each other, faith that we will take care of each other. Tribal cultures have more of an awareness of the ups and downs of life and a sense that other people are there to help. At some point all of us are going to be in a place where we're hurt and need our spirits to be lifted, and we will need help. The medicine that works then is kindness and sharing.

When I was a very young child, before I even went to school, my family visited the San Francisco Zoo. My maternal grandmother took me to say hello to a huge grizzly bear. She said, "That's your grandfather, the bear. You're Creek. You are bear clan." It made me feel there was no reason to be afraid and that there was a special protector for me.

When my younger brother and I went to school in the city, we were the only brown people there. My two other brothers were a little lighter than us, so they didn't get hassled. Sometimes strangers, usually male children and teenagers but also adult white men, would say horrible things to me because of the color of my skin. Discovering the cruelty of racism was very painful. That time would have been easier if my mother had been with us. She left when I was nine years old. For three years I didn't see her because my parents were angry at each other, but my grandparents would bring gifts and messages from my mother. My parents finally got a divorce and began to talk to each other. When I was twelve, we reconnected and began to visit again.

One of the reasons I initially went into teaching was that I didn't want Indian children to feel lonely. I did tutoring when I was on Alcatraz during the occupation of the island. My thought was that Indian children in the city need to have supportive people around them. I felt very lonely when I experienced childhood without a supportive community.

I never felt like I was part of the majority culture. As a physician, I have been educated in good schools and I can speak their language. I can go wherever I need to go in society and function in it, but my values feel different. Until recently I haven't had lasting relationships with people from that world. But when my first grandson was born, I realized he is part Santee Sioux, Filipino, Muscogee Creek, African American, Caucasian—and all human. It gets harder to think about people in categories supplied by the majority culture. I had to rethink culture, ethnicity, human values, and one human race. I can no longer make generalizations about "white culture," or use that vocabulary, because my grandson has grandmothers who are "white." And I wonder where their people came from before they were "white." Because I love my grandson, I have to see "white people" as human, even if some are unable to see me in the same way.

American culture encourages people to think of their value in terms of what they have accumulated or the potential they have to accumulate wealth. They think that if you have the ability to accumulate wealth, you can spare yourself pain, suffering, or difficult times. And they are disappointed because

every day is a good day

they keep buying and accumulating, and they're still in pain.

It is false to think that material things will bring happiness. And even in relationships, some people try to buy loyalty or affection. They think that because they have money, they should be able to buy kindness or respect. If one thinks of the world only in terms of what they can buy and their financial worth, then they would also have to purchase loyalty and trust. Trust is not based on ownership.

Mary and Carrie Dann

None of us spoke English when we started school. My oldest brother went away to a government boarding school. In boarding school they alter the mind, make changes, and program the students away from being Western Shoshone. They are very good at that. After boarding school, my brother went into World War II as a volunteer. He never spoke Shoshone when he came back. The loss of the language meant a loss of culture.

At one point some people kind of got lost. This had to do with them going to the government boarding schools where they were taught not to think Indian. Some of them left their homes when they were six years of age or younger, and they did not return until they were about eighteen years of age. When they came back, they were completely different people. They were no longer Western Shoshone. They were not traditional indigenous people. They were hollow.

I think we lost maybe a couple of generations of our people, and some of these lost people then became the so-called leaders of our nations. The boarding schools groomed these people for political leadership of their nations because the federal government knew they were no longer traditional people, no longer spiritual people. They were caught between two systems—the Western Shoshone beliefs and beliefs they were taught when they were forced to go to Christian churches.

To be a Western Shoshone is to be a person who understands who we are and where we come from. A Western Shoshone practices his or her own beliefs and ways and doesn't lose his or her language and culture. Before the

context is everything

coming of the United States, Indian people had their own laws. Our young people should look at these traditional laws and then try to live in a Western Shoshone way. I would like for young people to understand that our knowledge will not die out as long as there are enough of us to teach our children whatever little we know today. I would like for young people to be proud and respectful of one another, and of all people. That is the indigenous way.

Today we see too many of our young people who have lost respect for the Earth, the water, the air. All they want is to go out and make money. They are trying to find the American way of life, what they call the American dream, and when they are out there running after that money, they have no respect for anything else but getting that mighty dollar. That is not life.

Money is not the most important thing in the world. I would like our young people to know the meaning of Newe Segovia, Earth Mother, *and to be respectful toward the Earth and to everyone and everything else. Being respectful is important.*

Angela Gonzales

Some people want to emulate what they perceive to be Native American culture because they believe they have no culture of their own. When we discuss issues of identity and culture in my classes, I try to get students who don't feel they have their own culture to recall some particular family tradition or food dish, and in most cases they can recall something that is part of their family tradition. Social interaction around food is common to most cultures. At the end of the semester, we do an informal potluck dinner in my home. Everyone takes great pride in preparing and sharing a dish.

In Western culture, a college degree, especially from Harvard, confers social status on people. It is very hierarchical. It doesn't really matter where you get your degree from, what matters is what you do with it. I realize that my being able to get into a place like Harvard was a bit of sentimental tokenism. But once I got in, I had to really work hard. What I found at Hopi is that the degrees may close doors instead of open doors. Western education teaches you to argue, to evaluate, and to insist upon the rightness of your

every day is a good day

perspective. I don't think I have to unlearn all these things; I just need to learn to adapt them to situations at home. It is a tough balancing act.

There are a lot of questions about Indian identity in urban areas such as the San Francisco Bay Area where I used to live. As a consequence, I don't display my college degree on my office wall. Instead I display my certificate of tribal enrollment, because I have been challenged about my tribal identity. That was really a new experience for me. In an urban context, "Indian-ness" is defined by whether you are part of the Indian community. I have this sense of who I am as a Hopi, and yet that identity was being denied because I didn't meet this other person's criteria for what an Indian is.

I am really opposed to this idea of being either a.) Indian or b.) non-Indian. I think that it can always be a blending of the two cultures. You take what is good from both cultures and it makes you a better person.

Octaviana Valenzuela Trujillo

The major differentiating characteristic between tradition-oriented indigenous people and non-tradition oriented people, both indigenous and nonindigenous, is the nature of our spirituality, specifically the role it plays in determining our identity with regard to our way of life and orientation to the world. Though my professional career has focused on indigenous language, my greatest efforts have been explaining who we are as indigenous people. As an educator, this has involved countless hours promoting and defending Native educational methodology and curriculum. Even today, most professional educators have not been properly prepared to work with indigenous, or even culturally diverse, students. Contributing to this deficit in the education profession, our educational philosophy as indigenous people has not been adequately articulated for the general society, which still expects Native students to be educated with national cultural values that are often counter to Native values. Our schools, therefore, have failed to develop our Native human resources that are so vital for Nation building. We need to develop educational policies that respect and integrate indigenous philosophical perspectives.

context is everything

Joy Harjo

Colonization teaches us to hate ourselves. We are told that we are nothing until we adopt the ways of the colonizer, until we become the colonizer. But as Native people, we never fit into that system, and most of us have no wish to fit there. The tension of who we truly are and who we are forced to become is often unbearable and is the source of virulent self-hatred. I could see it in my father who, like so many Native people of his generation, drank to ease the pain of the disconnect from his culture and community. What I call the "overculture" is not a true culture; it is a pseudoculture. It does not grow human minds, hearts, and spirits. It is in place to steal. The overriding values are based on material ownership, which confers power. But what kind of power is that? It is transitory and violent. Humans are separated by competition and failure, instead of being gathered together.

My experiences are different because I sometimes go unrecognized as Indian in a crowd. It all depends on the context, the community. I am light-skinned, but my Muscogee Creek identity was something I did not question at all. There was not a problem fitting into my community at home or when I was away from home at Indian school. There was no question within me or my family or my community. It was never a personal issue until I became involved with a Pueblo man from New Mexico. Suddenly, I was "that white woman" or "that hippie." This was a shock to me and engendered much shame. I was Muscogee Creek, and had been all my life, and I did not have questions regarding my identity.

The most embarrassing incident happened about fifteen years ago. Even now as I recall it, I feel a flush of frustration and shame creep up my back. I was an invited guest for a coming-of-age ceremony for a friend's daughter. This was the first time this ceremony had been performed in that Arizona tribe for many years. It was quite an event with a huge feast. I was beckoned to eat, and as I followed the crowd to the table, a woman was disciplining her child with a warning that the white person over there was going to come and get him and take him away. I looked behind me to see the white person who the mother was using as an example. It was me. It was one of the worst moments of my life. Even now, I wrestle with the telling because it takes away from the larger story I wish to tell of our people—meaning all indigenous peoples—for whom my life is dedicated. In that story I am included. In that story, all of our experiences have worth. So my question is, "What does this story tell about us?"

I have also had the opposite experience. Once in Oregon, when I was leaving one of the first Native drama group performances, I had rocks thrown at me because I am Indian. In Oklahoma, I have been refused service in a restaurant for being Indian, and also in Oklahoma, I have had my word doubted by a policeman whom I saw write "Indian" across the report. And the police refused to take action.

Joanne Shenandoah

Our path is very simple and clear. It seems the larger society tends to focus on the outer self while we are taught from a young age to focus on the inner self. There is also an unhealthy emphasis on ownership, control, and every "man" for himself. I realize many people are searching for who they really are and where they belong or what they are supposed to be doing with their lives. They don't have a sense of identity, belonging, continuity. For example, thousands of women and men increasingly resort to surgery to enhance their outer self to defy aging, but the most attractive people I have ever met are elders who have grown into beautiful souls.

While in the midst of realizing "the American dream" with fourteen years in the computer industry as a systems integration design engineer, I found myself sitting in my big office staring out my window as tree cutters were about to destroy a huge two-hundred-year-old tree. As I watched that awful process, I felt like I was also being uprooted. At that moment I realized I was not fulfilling my responsibilities on the Earth. Everyone has a special gift or talent that can be used to benefit the larger community. The land at Oneida was calling for me to come home. I turned down a guaranteed salary of $250,000 per year plus incentive bonuses that wasn't even remotely appealing. I was on another journey. I wanted to come home and I wanted to

context is everything

sing, which was my natural talent and gift.

My Native name is Tekaliwahh:kwa which means "she sings." This name was given to me as a young girl long before I became a musician. Our Iroquois elders know we have specific duties on the Earth, and I was not ful-filling them while living in Maryland. So I moved back to Oneida Territory in 1990 and began a career in music.

My immediate family has been incredibly supportive of my career. I firmly believe in the family, the basic circle of life that determines all our lives. In the Haudenosaunee way, it is natural to affirm the family circle and to express our deepest gratitude for the infinite goodness of being.

Nowhere is the Haudenosaunee appreciation for women better reflected than in their music and dance. When the women dance, they form a circle around the drum; they move with the Earth, counterclockwise, their feet caressing the Earth as they shuffle to one of the hundreds of verses sung in their honor. To be part of that circle is a great source of strength for me.

Jaune Quick-to-See Smith

The government and the outer community accuse Indian people of losing their culture because they don't speak their language or dress every day in traditional clothing or look like the Italians who play Indians in the movies. Whites don't dress in pilgrim clothing either and are not readily identifiable as Greek or Portuguese or English or Irish. Why then do they insist that all American Indians should look alike or that they can readily identify who is Indian and who is not? Can we readily identify who is Irish?

Culture is not race and race is not culture. They can both apply at the same time but not necessarily. Indian people who are adopted away from their tribe and grow up exclusively with whites know nothing of Indian culture. Their Indian blood will not come to the fore and teach them culture. On the other hand, Mrs. Grounds, a well-known, respected elder at Blackfeet who lived into old age and had many Blackfeet great-grandchildren, was white. She fell off a wagon train as a baby, and the Blackfeet took her in.

every day is a good day

Raised with the Blackfeet, she became steeped in the culture and was considered an expert on the culture.

Many say that loss of language is loss of one's culture, and there is truth in that. Linguistic experts say the genetic imprint is so strong that it can last for three generations. Interestingly, those of us who were forbidden to speak our own languages by the government pronounce our English with breath sounds. We may not master the glottal stops (click) or the fricatives (breath), but we often construct English sentences with adjectives and adverbs placed in sequence as in our traditional language. Though language carries a lot of cultural information, there are other facets to culture, such as slang, humor, gestures, dance, music, art, literature, taboos, and more.

More than anything, Indian humor works in English too. Recently, an e-mail was distributed around Indian Country entitled "the Bureau of Iraqi Affairs," which parodied the Bureau of Indian Affairs. The newly formed Bureau of Iraqi Affairs issued a directive that English would be the official language now, and if Iraqi people didn't speak English, a translator fluent in German would be provided. It further provided that hospitals would be issued such critical supplies as Band-Aids, burn cream, and duct tape. Our humor definitely expresses who we are. It may not make sense to outsiders or it may seem too bleak, but it does make sense to us in its irony.

As an artist, I am particularly interested in how we express ourselves visually. I'm also interested in our traditional art from the past or the present and how it relates to our contemporary art. I find no difficult gaps between these various art forms like the anthropologists do. Art taught at home often follows more obvious constructs than university-taught art. All of it is about expressing one's life experience and thankfulness. In my travels through Indian Country there are always stories describing the process and its import to the artist, whether college trained or tribally trained. The importance is in the process, not the final product. Like meditation or chanting or drumming or prayer, the process of making art is thankfulness, and it keeps the artist balanced and healthy.

When we were planning our tribal museum, I traveled by car across three states with elders, an architect, the museum director, and tribal

context is everything

traditionalists to view other tribal museums. It was a wonderful time of story-telling, discoveries, old memories, and education. We were starting from scratch with no building, no collections. I located a collection that belonged to a potato magnate who supplied potatoes to McDonald's. I knew Simplot would want to do the right thing by providing us with some items for our museum. Wrong. So the elders told me not to worry: "Those old things have lost their power when the whites take them. We don't know where they've been. We'll make new things." Oh, Indian survival is wonderful, an art in itself.

Lurline Wailana McGregor

My father was Hawaiian, Chinese, and Scottish and my mother is from Indianapolis of German ancestry. My parents met on the SS Lurline, the premier ocean liner that used to cross the Pacific between Honolulu and the West Coast. My mother was visiting Hawai'i, and my father was returning home. After my mother finished college, they married and settled in Honolulu. I am the only daughter of five children, and as they promised each other, they named me Lurline.

I grew up in a multicultural household, which is characteristic of many Hawaiian families and is what we call "local" in Hawai'i. There are very few pure Hawaiians left, and they tend to live in the more rural parts of Hawai'i (not Honolulu) and have more traditional lifestyles. I think my father struggled with balancing the two worlds of the more traditional household that he grew up in and the much more Westernized family environment in which I grew up. Since my father was an attorney, a judge, a politician, and a businessman during his career, his success depended on his ability to think, act, and talk like his peers. As we were growing up, he made sure he taught us how to act properly around haoles (white people). We went to nice restaurants to practice our manners. At the same time, in the home and around family we did traditional things and ate food that was Hawaiian, although I never realized that what we were doing was Hawaiian until I got older and started distinguishing among the different cultures. The

every day is a good day

one thing really missing, though, was the language, and I'm sure my father grew up with his parents speaking Hawaiian in the home, but he never spoke to us in Hawaiian except for words here and there. Yet his heart was pure Hawaiian, and I know he loved his culture. He never missed an opportunity to help another Hawaiian, whether it was helping them enroll their children in Kamehameha schools or giving them free legal services.

Although my work and urban lifestyle require me to participate in a Western culture and therefore acquiesce to certain Western values in order to be successful (not unlike how my father had to act), I am personally motivated by the ideals of my own culture. Western goals of materialism and accumulation of power for its own sake do not particularly drive me. At the end of the day, my satisfaction comes from feeling that I've done something to help the community.

It is very difficult to be Hawaiian today and to hold onto those things that sometimes are in direct conflict with trying to survive in a Western culture. Land in Hawai'i is the most valuable asset we have, which is why foreigners even to this day come to Hawai'i wanting what's left of our land. Hawaiians are often the last people who can afford to own land. If you cannot live off the land because you have no land to live off of, then what's left? Moving to Honolulu, living in an apartment, and working at a minimum-wage job? Many people tolerate it because it is their life outside their jobs that fulfills them. Others leave Hawai'i altogether.

Thirty years ago we as a generation started to understand everything we were losing and made a commitment to turn things around. Today Hawaiian language is flourishing in the schools, Hawaiian chant and hula is strong, there are many beautiful new songs being created every day, and many Hawaiians are actively participating in cultural activities. Unfortunately, there still is the issue of the economics, and that isn't necessarily getting better. We are way overrepresented in all the negative socioeconomic statistics. It can be very difficult to fit in.

context is everything

LaDonna Harris

Some people say we live in two worlds: one white, one Native. I live in one world; that of a Comanche woman. No matter where I am or who I am with, I filter everything through my Comanche values.

The main difference I see between the larger society and being Comanche is the value we place on our kinship system. We have a sense of responsibility to one another, and it is reciprocal. Even in the ancient Comanche way, these kinship relationships did not have to be blood kin. The relationships were established and maintained on the basis of what you did for one another. They were based on reciprocity. We even think about animals, the Earth, the Sun, in relational terms, in kinships terms. And when one thinks of others in kinship terms, one has a responsibility for them.

Within that kinship system and frame of reference, we don't accumulate material wealth for ourselves; we accumulate things so we can do well for others. The Comanche have a very flat society. The more honored and privileged you are, the more you have to give back. It is your responsibility to redistribute what you have. In the old ways, most tribal cultures had giveaways, potlatches, or other forms of redistributing their wealth. Giveaways are a form of honoring, and they help keep the community level so that one group or set of families will not be on a higher economic scale than the others. In contemporary times we still give away material goods, but we also give away knowledge, ideas, and resources. It is important to find ways to fit traditional values into our contemporary lives. I sift everything through my Comanche values, and if I can't understand it within the context of my Comanche values or it doesn't feel right, it sends up a huge red flag. When I have tried to push my traditional values behind me, I have been less successful. I do well when I am just myself, a Comanche woman. Our young people are trying to figure out how to continue to maintain their traditional values when they live and work away from their communities. It drives me crazy when people say we have to live in two worlds. We can't live in two worlds. We have to live in one world and carry those values with us and live them every day wherever we live. People become dysfunctional when they

every day is a good day

adopt situational values. You can't live one way in a tribal community and then go out of the community and have a totally different set of values. One has to be creative and think about how to continue to hold onto their traditional values, to be sharing, to be respectful no matter where they are.

I was raised by my grandparents, along with my parents. What I learned from my grandmother is that we are not victims. As a proud Comanche girl, I thought I could do anything. I think some of our people have been trapped in a victimization mentality for generations, and they then unwittingly become victims of their own victimization and can't stop the behavior. We are capable people who can do anything we set our minds to do.

Gail Small

Austin Two Moons used to tell me that the Cheyenne have never lived anything but war. The war today is against giant energy companies who want to ravish our reservation. Yet we find moments of joy and beauty that give us strength to keep on. Recently several generations of Cheyenne people gathered to share fellowship and to honor the memory of a young Cheyenne man who was killed in a highway accident. We had the memorial at Old Man Whitedirt's place. It may be one of the last old time giveaways we will ever see. They turned a beautiful three-year-old horse loose and whoever caught it could take it home and keep it. A young Cheyenne cowboy from Tongue River caught the horse. They also gave away five tipis with poles, about thirty star quilts, twenty Pendleton blankets, and about ten tables loaded with goods. They even gave away a complete drum set with another Pendleton blanket. They honored his five living grandmothers. It was a sight to see the grandmothers all dancing to a beautiful honor song. Only one of them was on a walker. The rest were dancing. The Cheyenne people relish these occasions when they can experience traditional practices and enjoy the tremendous strength and sense of community that has kept the Cheyenne strong.

context is everything

Sarah James

The main difference between us and people in the larger society is that indigenous people have a home, a homeland we share with people we are related to. We also have a common knowledge and understanding of oral history. The Creator put us where we are to take care of this part of the world. Nonindigenous people are newcomers to this part of the world, the Western Hemisphere. Some are invaders; some come in a respectful way. They originated from some other place. They need to have a respect for our people and the land, learn our ways, and learn how to take care this part of world, our part of the world. I believe there are now more respectful nonindigenous people because they are learning about the Earth and what is happening to the Earth.

Our people feel a responsibility to the land, the people, and to themselves. We believe our people should be healthy and have a clean mind, in order to think clearly, and a strong body. But now our people are dying from alcohol, drugs, and a lot of new diseases. At one time our people were healthy and did not know anything about greed. We used to own very little and carry everything that we owned on our backs. What little we had, we shared with one another. Still today we share our food, our clothing, our time, our knowledge.

There are so many chemicals in the food, it causes confusion in the mind and body. And people don't get enough exercise. Before white people came, we were nomadic people who traveled long distances and ate very little. Our people could remain strong enough to walk in snowshoes for days without getting tired by using their knowledge of how to pace themselves, balance fluid intake, and breathe in the cold air. People cannot contribute to the community or to a healthy Earth if they are not healthy themselves. To have a good life, it is important to drink and eat in moderation, and to know the difference between greed and need. Too much waste and greed has damaged the Earth. We have to give up some things in order to balance the environment. We have to learn to share more, to reuse, recycle, and use less energy.

Global warming is a very real threat to us here in the north. Though our land is one of the few places on Earth where the natural ecosystem still works, we will be affected first by the holes in the ozone layers. Pollution and the destruction of the world's natural ecosystems will eventually harm everyone. So protecting the environment and the Arctic National Wildlife Refuge is everybody's responsibility, not just the indigenous people.

We must all work together in balance with each other. We must educate all people about respect for who we are and respect for our Earth. We must work hard to know our non-Native friends. It is so important to find the common ground of all people. Some people think this is so hard to do because we come from many diverse cultures. But we must only look down and see that we are standing on the same ground. We drink the same water, breathe the same air, and want to eat healthy food. We all have children, and we want them to survive in a healthy and just world.

Florence Soap

Stories are very important to Cherokee people. Stories have always played a big part in my life. When we were little, we played near a big cave near the water but we were not allowed go back into that cave. Once near the cave we found safety pins, pottery, little bitty plates, and things that belonged to the Little People who lived in those caves. Lots of times people use spirit protection to protect the house so the Little People won't come. We used to live in a house where Little People would rattle the pots and pans unless we left food out for them. When we left food out for them, they left the pots and pans alone.

There is a story about an older couple who lived up in the hills by Evansville Creek. They had a little girl. The Little People took the little girl. The family and a lot of other people looked for her but could never find her. One day they came upon a very rocky area near the water and they found the little girl sitting very near the stream. She did not want to go home. It is believed that she was in the company of the Little People. She chose to stay with them, but her parents brought her home anyway.

context is everything

Shortly thereafter, she died.

We did not have sweat lodges, but we did have a plant with leaves like tobacco that they would put under a blanket, roll you up in the blanket, and then heat the blanket to make you sweat and purify you. Also I remember when I was a girl, they would sit us on a chair or lay us on the floor and cover us with a blanket and place a medicine plant and a pot of hot coals under the blanket to make us sweat and purify us. It is a good medicine. If that same plant is kept for one to two years, it can be boiled and drunk to cure a cough. We are losing a lot of our ways and a lot of knowledge is being lost when the older people leave. We can ask God to help us retain our ways.

Rosalie Little Thunder

We are all human beings. What then brought us to this point where we are so far apart in history and in values? At some point back there in European evolution (or in their own stories) they determined that their way of life was right and that they were superior. That is where our paths diverged. My grandfather made a simple observation: "Tuwa wichaka keya wichagna cha," meaning someone fooled them that they were right. This way of thinking probably inhibited their ability to learn about us. I am greatly distraught by all the energy our people waste on Western education when we already have the wisdom of teaching, learning, and living in a good way.

Wahwayela opiic'iya is a valued behavior among traditional Lakota. I will make an effort to translate, though my English is limited. It means that one doesn't splash onto the scene, but observes quietly and then integrates one's behavior to fit the situation without compromising their own character. When that is compared with the Euro-American need to always be right, to control, and to have everything validated by their own science, one can begin to see why there are such differences between tradition-oriented indigenous peoples and white people.

My first language is Lakota, and I have taught the language all of my adult life. It is within the Lakota language that I find the knowledge to

every day is a good day

view the world as our ancestors must have seen it, in a holistic way. I am an artist and also research historical Lakota art, which provides a window to my ancestors' way of thinking and living.

My thoughts are occupied by the damage to the land and threatened wildlife. We live in a society that is wasteful and disposes of everything, without even giving it a thought. We can buy plastic things by the truckload. My parents and grandparents made use of everything, even tin cans and empty thread spools. They were environmentally economical when they carefully repaired things and used them again and again.

In March 1997, I was arrested at Yellowstone National Park, where I had gone with a Lakota spiritual leader and others to pray for the buffalo that were being slaughtered by the Department of Agriculture and Livestock. The decimation of the buffalo in Yellowstone struck deeply in my heart and tested my spirituality. It is the first time that I felt collective grief. I felt as if I was grieving beyond that time and beyond myself, not just for losses and trauma in my little short life.

After my arrest, some people commented about my bravery and courage. At that time, I sure wasn't feeling very brave. I was cold, tired, hungry, and very scared as I watched a front-end loader dragging around the steaming buffalo carcasses. There was even a moving fetus. Tasangt'a, or "stunned spirit," is my best description for the way I was feeling. I wish I could understand the view-point of the Department of Livestock agents. One minute they were shouting at us, somewhat belligerently, and then they became silent as they scrambled for their vehicles and left hurriedly, bumping over the prairie where there were no roads. Months later, I spoke with a neighboring rancher who had a close view of the scene, and he too said he often wondered what the Department of Livestock agents saw that day. They were looking beyond me, not at me.

My feelings and actions continue to be dictated by a need to repair the damage. I use the term "miners' canary" to describe the role of the buffalo as an indicator of a damaged ecosystem. It seems that indigenous people are also "miners' canaries" for humanity, though we are viewed as a problem to be solved, not keepers of essential Earth wisdom.

context is everything

So much has happened to contribute to my learning these past few years. This knowledge is there for all of us if we are receptive to becoming connected to and responsible for the sacred beings that are all around us. I believe sacrifice, humility, and suffering provides access to this related-ness. Our people used to live on the edge of survival, always in extreme hardship. As a walking culture, they were so close to everything in the natural world. They knew all of their relatives in the natural world inti-mately and depended on the spirits of the ancestors to survive. Their prayers, which arose from pain and suffering, were the sincerest form of prayer. They found beauty in hardship and expressed their reverence in their art. They composed ceremonial songs in the face of the cold, biting north wind—songs of gratitude and humility.

governance:
the people and the land

Chapter Four

*Sovereignty is the ability to carry
out your own direction. If you think
sovereign, you can be sovereign.*
—Audrey Shenandoah, Onondaga

Much of the work of contemporary tribal leaders can be characterized as a fight for the right to "freely pursue, their economic, social, and cultural development," the United Nations definition of self-determination. But many leaders spend a considerable amount of time answering very basic questions about tribal governments such as, "Why do tribal governments continue to exist?" Many people don't realize that tribal governments predate the U.S. government, and that there is a lengthy history of government-to-government relations between the United States and indigenous nations. Most of the so-called great Indian wars were about indigenous people fighting for the right to be self governing and to retain their ancestral lands. LaDonna Harris says, "Some people view tribal governments as 'play' governments because they learned nothing at all about them in high school or in political science classes. We have kept our cultural and political autonomy, and few people understand that."

It its early history, the fledgling U.S. recognized sovereignty in formal treaties with indigenous nations. Between 1779, when the Delaware signed the first peace treaty with the United States, and 1871, when the treaty-making era ended, the United States executed and the Senate ratified 370 formal treaties with Native nations. Though treaties were and are recognized as valid legal instruments and statements of federal policy, they have rarely been honored by the United States.

In an effort to protect their lands and people, many tribal leaders sent delegations to meet with the English, Spanish, French, and later the U.S. governments. Traveling to foreign lands with a trusted interpreter, tribal ambassadors took painstakingly drawn maps of their lands to show heads of other governments. They also took along gifts, letters, and proclamations. Though tribal leaders thought they were being dealt with as heads of state and as equals, historical records indicate they were objects of curiosity, and there was a great deal of disdain, ridicule, and overt racism toward these earnest delegates.

The fight to retain tribal sovereignty remains a high priority for the more than 500 federally recognized nations, tribes, bands, and villages in the U.S. Faith Smith says, "Sovereignty is the right to define the present and the future as a people." Joanne Shenandoah says, "Sovereignty means self-governance, and that governance is only as good as the people who are involved. It is the people, especially those who carry the medicine, speak the language, and carry on the traditions. A land claim is not just about acreage. It is sacred ground where generations before us sang, danced, and held ceremonies. The land is the point of life."

Land is critical to the cultural survival of these communities. The Dann sisters describe sovereignty as, "The lands upon which we had our freedom before the coming of white people; the lands upon which our forefathers walked, cherished, and took care of—that is the whole Western Shoshone country, and not just what the American government refers to as Indian Country. That is sovereignty." According to the

First Nations Development Institute, by the early twentieth century the United States took more than 2 billion acres of land held by indigenous people either by treaty or agreement or by official government confiscation with no remuneration whatsoever. Many federal land policies further reduced tribal land holdings. The 1887 Dawes Allotment Act set the stage for breaking up commonly held tribal lands. Cherokee people, who had always held lands in common, were devastated by the individual allotment of lands. Today, the land base of indigenous nations ranges from the vast Navajo Nation—which spans parts of several states—to some tiny reserves of less than twenty acres. Collectively, tribal governments now hold more than 50 million acres of land, a tiny fraction of their original land holdings.

Some tribal governments, such as the Onondaga, continue their original form of government and even issue their own passports for international travel, while some of the California rancherias (small reservations) must fight for federal recognition after centuries of outrageous exploitation. Tribal governments are formed in many different ways—some according to ancient tribal traditions, others as an adaptation of traditional governments. For example, some Pueblo leaders are selected by gifted spiritual people, while the neighboring Diné (Navajo) Nation selects its leaders by popular vote.

In the Cherokee Nation, the current system of tribal government bears little resemblance to traditional governance, which was a system of semi-autonomous communities. Leaders of all the Cherokee people were necessary only in times of catastrophe or when the people had to defend themselves from an external threat. In historic Cherokee times, no single leader would have the unilateral authority of a present-day principal chief. But no matter what form contemporary tribal governments take, the spirit of sovereignty survives, even among those people who have lost much of their ancestral land and rights. Native Hawaiians in particular are waging an inspiring battle to retain their rights to some of the most coveted land in the Western Hemisphere. In 1999, Ingrid Washinawatok El-Issa, a Menominee indigenous rights activist, said, "Since the time that

governance

human beings offered thanks for the first sunrise, sovereignty has been an integral part of indigenous peoples' daily existence. Sovereignty is that wafting thread securing the components of a society. Sovereignty runs through the vertical strands and secures the entire pattern. That is the fabric of Native society."

Though protecting tribal sovereignty is a priority, indigenous communities face a daunting set of critical social and economic issues, including double-digit unemployment, poor housing, and epidemic health problems such as diabetes. And tribal governments face continual attempts to further erode their remaining rights: for example, powerful mining and oil and gas companies want to exploit tribal lands for marketable natural resources and extremists argue that indigenous people should not have "special rights" to their own governments. But often the opposition is their old foe—state governments. The stress between state and tribal governments continues unabated as the two grapple with issues of jurisdiction, law enforcement, and taxation.

The debate over economic development initiatives is not always external. In some instances, the internal debate has created deep division, even among families. Faced with rapidly declining federal support for core social programs and few alternatives for economic development, some tribal governments have endorsed the wholesale extraction of natural resources from their lands, and in a couple of cases, the storage of toxic waste, all of which stimulates considerable debate within their communities. And like some state governments, a number of indigenous nations have built impressive casino operations thereby making major contributions to the economy of their neighboring communities. While the casinos undoubtedly give tribal governments unprecedented economic and political power and generate much-needed income for schools, education scholarships, health care, housing, and other desperately needed services, some people still question the eventual impact of casinos on the social and cultural web of the community. Jaune Quick-to-See Smith says, "Some people excuse casinos by saying that Indians have always had traditional gambling games. The fact is that modern casino gambling is driven by economic desperation, not tradition. Flathead stick games or Northern Piegan feather games or any other tribal gambling game is about cultural bonding. The process teaches cultural social interactions and real skill. The process is equally as important as the end result. This is not the case in casino gambling, which is an individual activity with one goal, and any skill is demolished by odds for the house.

My biggest concern is not about the gambling issue itself but about the reductive effect it has on the sovereign power of our treaties. It's a catch-22 situation. The tribes are damned if they do and damned if they don't. Damned if they don't share with their state and community. But damned if they do share any monies with states and communities. Negotiations that result in money, even a penny, given over to the states erode our sovereignty. We can't afford to allow any more threats to our sovereignty at this point. No matter what our economic resources are, from here on out, the states will be asking for a handout." And Joanne Shenandoah asks, "Are we willing to sell away rights promised to us in 1794 just to have alcohol or slot machines in the casinos?"

LaDonna Harris says, "We are moving so rapidly. We are in a unique period of time. If you look at our economic and political growth in a historical context, it is clear that we almost bottomed out in the nineteenth century. Then there was a period of revival, particularly after the 1960s, when there was tremendous growth. If you add in the revenue from the casinos, the growth is just off the chart. If you look at the rapid advancements that have been made both socially and politically, it creates some internal turmoil."

Others argue that the jobs created and income generated by tribal gaming greatly outweighs any potential negative impact. The inspirational story of the rebirth and revitalization of the Pequot Nation, symbolized by the opening of a grand museum in 1998, was made possible by revenue from operation of the largest Native American casino in North America. And in Oklahoma, tribal gaming operations have agreed to contribute almost $100 million in revenue to the public school systems and millions more to other services and programs benefiting both tribal and nontribal citizens. The debate over using gaming to generate income for tribal and state governments will continue as more cash-strapped state governments and tribal governments seek revenue to pay for essential services.

Tribal governments and communities also face many other challenges. On the Northern Cheyenne Reservation in Montana, Gail Small, a gifted and dedicated Cheyenne lawyer, has been working for decades—literally since she was in high school—to protect Cheyenne lands from the energy giants that surround her homelands. The legal framework for Cheyenne sovereignty is supposed to protect the Northern Cheyenne, but there is a very real danger that their beloved homelands will be drained of groundwater by irresponsible coal-bed methane gas drilling. When I think of Gail, I have an image of a beautiful, strong Cheyenne woman with her finger in the dike, alone but resolute. Gail once told me that the Cheyenne people have always had to fight for everything they have. When they face a particularly tough battle, they remember that not many people in this country or anywhere in the world can say they defeated the United States in military battle, as the Cheyenne did at the Battle of Little Big Horn. Regrettably, they will have to continue to fight for a long time to come.

Wilma Mankiller

Though I have lived most of my life on my grandfather's Cherokee land allotment in rural Adair County, Oklahoma, I learned a great deal about indigenous people, governance, and land during the twenty years I spent in the San Francisco Bay Area. Soon after my Native American brothers and sisters joined the occupation of Alcatraz Island in late 1969, I made plans to visit the island. The morning I made the short journey to Alcatraz, my heart and mind made a quantum leap forward.

Lady dawn descended on the nearly empty streets of Fisher-

every day is a good day

man's Wharf, bearing the gift of a brand-new day. Fishing boats rocked in their slips, awaiting the day's journey, as shop owners sleepily prepared for the onslaught of tourists. An occasional foghorn or the barking of a stray dog was the only sound other than the steady lap of the ocean against the docks. Alcatraz Island, several miles across San Francisco Bay, was barely visible as I boarded a boat for the former military and federal prison, which had recently been taken over by indigenous people and declared "Indian Land." Mist and fog gave the island a dreamlike quality that seemed fitting for a place where the American dream was rejected and an Indigenous dream declared.

The young students who occupied Alcatraz Island claimed that federal surplus lands such as Alcatraz should be returned to tribal peoples on legal and moral ground, and that treaties, land rights, and tribal sovereignty should be respected and honored. This was not the first relationship between indigenous people and Alcatraz. Long before Europeans arrived, Ohlones and other indigenous people of the coast rested and got their bearings on Alcatraz Island, called the Island of the Pelicans (Isla de los Alcatraces) after the seabirds that gathered there. In the late nineteenth century, Modocs and other tribal people were imprisoned at Alcatraz for fighting the United States Army in a desperate attempt to retain their ancestral homelands. When the Spanish first settled in the mid-1700s on the land that is today California, there were more than 275,000 indigenous people living there. That changed very quickly. By 1900, fewer than 16,000 indigenous people remained. It is a miracle that even that many survived. Indigenous people of California endured widespread violence, starvation, disease, genocide, rape, and slavery. As late as 1870, a few communities in California were still paying bounties for Indian scalps or severed heads. One hundred years later, the descendants of some of the indigenous people who survived the conquerors, miners, and settlers joined others at Alcatraz to find their bearings just as their ancestors had done so long ago.

I visited Alcatraz several times during the nineteen-month occupation of the island. At any given time, the Alcatraz community

governance

was composed of an eclectic group of indigenous people, activists, civil rights veterans, students, and people who just wanted to be at a "happening." Richard Oakes, a visionary young Mohawk who emerged as an early spokesman for the Alcatraz occupiers, said, "There are many old prophecies that speak of the younger people rising up and finding a way for the People to live." (In their own languages, many tribes call themselves by words that mean "the People.") Alcatraz was a catalyst for many young people who would spend their lives forging a new path for the People.

The Alcatraz experience was certainly a watershed for me. The leaders articulated principles and ideas I had thought about but could not name or articulate. During the Alcatraz occupation and that period of activism, anything seemed possible. Inspired by Alcatraz, I began a four-year association with the Pit River Tribe, which was involved in a legal and political struggle to regain their ancestral lands near Mount Shasta. Mostly I worked as a volunteer at the tribe's legal offices in San Francisco, but I frequently visited Pit River lands, where I learned about the history of indigenous people in California from traditional leaders. Occasionally one of the leaders would bring out an old cardboard box filled with tribal documents supporting their land claims. They treated the precious documents almost as sacred objects. At Pit River, I learned that sovereignty was more than a legal concept. It represents the ability of the People to articulate their own vision of the future, control their destiny, and watch over their lands. It means freedom and responsibility.

Another place that had a great impact on me was the Oakland Intertribal Friendship House, which served as an oasis for a diverse group of indigenous people living in a busy urban area far from their home communities. We gathered there for dinners, meetings, and to listen to a wonderful array of speakers, including Tom Porter, a Mohawk leader who spoke about his people's fight to remain separate and independent. He explained that the Mohawk's 1795 treaty with the United States provided that they had the "perpetual right to live on their reservations in independent sovereignty, never to be disturbed." He spoke movingly about the important role women play among his people. He said that traditional Iroquois women selected the chiefs and could depose them if they did not perform their duties properly. The speech had a powerful, lasting impact on me.

My experiences at Alcatraz and Pit River led me to cofound, with Joe Carillo, California Indians for a Fair Settlement, which encouraged California tribal people to reject a proposed settlement of all land claims for only pennies per acre. All this work helped me to understand more fully the historical context in which tribal people live our contemporary lives.

In 1976 I was further galvanized by a treaty conference at the Standing Rock Sioux Reservation in Wakpala, South Dakota, that readied delegates for the 1977 United Nations Conference on Indigenous Rights in Geneva. I had been working as a volunteer to help indigenous people prepare for the Geneva conference by documenting the fact that from the time of initial contact with Europeans, tribal communities were treated as separate nations, and numerous agreements between the emerging United States and tribal nations were signed.

At Wakpala, tribal sovereignty was framed as an issue of international significance. The concept of self-determination in international law as defined by UN General Assembly Resolution 1514 resonates with indigenous people: "All peoples have the right to self-determination. By virtue of that right they freely determine their political status and freely pursue their economic, social, and cultural development."

During this time, I also came to understand that among some tribal people, including the Cherokee, there was a historical period when there was little separation between political and spiritual organizations. Cherokee spiritual leaders were involved in conducting the council meetings that provided some of the political structure whereby major decisions were made by the entire settlement. Council meetings were often held after or during ceremonies, which helped prepare the

governance

people to deal with major issues affecting the community. However, in contemporary times, there is a formal separation between the political organization and spiritual practitioners.

The Alcatraz, Pit River, California Indian for a Fair Settlement, and the treaty Conference experiences were great preparation for my future role as principal chief of the Cherokee Nation.

The Gathering
Linda Aranaydo

In a way, people think of sovereignty as an abstract concept. I think of it in terms of a mother taking care of a family. But sometimes sovereignty means people huffing and puffing about who is in charge. Whoever is in charge needs to be sure to take care of our babies, take care of our elders, the communities, keep us together, and make us be good humans. If sovereignty is something that leads us to be better human beings, then I'm all for it. But sovereignty shouldn't be just a way to become more materialistic. The money from the casinos should be going to take care of the people and to create healthy, vibrant human communities. Leaders should look forward to future generations and not take their images of leadership from the American materialistic culture. Tribal leaders should not be motivated by personal gain, or gain only for their supporters.

Beatrice Medicine

When they put us on reservations, the tiospaye, *or extended family systems, were disrupted, though* tiospaye *still has meaning among the more tradition-oriented people. It is not related to clan. A clan is a named unit from a mythical ancestor. Members of clans believe they are descended from a bear or other totemic figure. Tiospaye is a larger unit, though both clans and the* tiospaye *can regulate marriage. We have to reteach that family system to our people. The Lakota Nation, or the Oyate, is a distinct nation of relatives with their own language, culture, and belief system. It is part of a larger grouping of the seven bands of the Sioux, some of whom got together at the Sun Dance, a ritual in the summer. We had a certain way of governance and a value system that allowed us to be a self-governing body. The older people still see it that way, and some younger leaders are looking to them to understand the notion of nationhood.*

LaDonna Harris

We are the only people in the United States who can rethink how we want to govern ourselves. We need to clearly define our values and decide how we can structure those values within our government. Our value system needs to be incorporated into our governmental systems and constitutions. Our governments should incorporate respect for one another and a willingness to listen to all viewpoints before making an important decision. We should find ways to reinforce generosity, honoring of each other, redistribution of resources, and helping one another.

Faith Smith

We have our own governments. Sovereignty means the right to define the present and the future as a people. I do not feel included in the U.S. founding documents. Growing up, even Indian kids are taught to feel warm and fuzzy over the Declaration of Independence and to stand up and put their hands on their hearts. We have to do a kind of remedial education with ourselves.

governance

Joanne Shenandoah

*I understand that the indigenous interpretation of sovereignty is
neither absolute nor fixed, but a free-flowing concept that involves many
elements, the most important of which is our responsibility to act as custodi-
ans of the natural world in trust for other species and those yet unborn.*

*Our respective governments fit the international definitions of
nation-states in that we had set territories, governing bodies, distinct identi-
ties, languages, and cultures. Also, we exercised active jurisdiction over our
lands to the exclusion of other nations. But with this authority came great
responsibility, which, if violated, could result in the extinguishment of our
national rights. For instance, if a nation acted in an environmentally irresponsible way that brought harm to the Earth and placed the well-being of
animals, plants, and humans at risk, its authority could be removed and the
nation displaced. So too, if a nation disrupted the regional peace by acting
in a belligerent manner of becoming involved in the marketing or trading of
land in exchange for wealth, then the leadership could be removed. Sovereignty was never rigid or absolute but subject to international law as defined
by multinational aboriginal assemblies such as the Haudenosaunee Grand
Council, the Powhatan Confederacy, or the Wabanaki Confederacy.*

*My mother, Maisie Shenandoah, Wolf Clan Mother of the Oneida
Nation, gathered together a group of families to build up our territory on
what is known today as the "thirty-two acres" in the city of Oneida, New
York. It was the dream of her mother, Mary Cornelius Winder, to reunite the
Oneidas. She and her sister, Delia Waterman, worked tirelessly for years to
initiate one of the largest land claims in the United States. Ms. Waterman
is now 102. These women and the majority of Oneidas wanted to revive
the ancestral government, which consists of nine* rotiiane *(male leaders),
nine female leaders (Clan Mothers), and eighteen Faith Keepers (a male
and female spiritual adviser for each* rotiine-*Clan Mother). Each traditional
leader had to have qualities such as humility, patience, a good command
of our language, and knowledge of our spiritual beliefs, since they had to
conduct our ceremonies. All leaders were selected by clan, endorsed by the*

*people, and expected to abide by a strict moral code. This council, which
exists among the Oneidas of Southwold, Ontario, was to help restore
democracy to the Oneidas and to revive our spiritual rituals. That did
not happen. Instead the Oneida Nation of New York, Inc., and a "men's
council" is recognized by the United States government as the official Oneida
government. This very government has suspended the membership rights of
Delia Waterman, a centenarian without whom the Oneida Nation of New
York would not exist.*

*My standing and benefits as an Oneida human being were stripped
away in 1995 for going out on a march for democracy. The suspension took
place without due process of any kind. How many years will our people have
to suffer because the Bureau of Indian Affairs decided to create and empower
a "sovereign" nation that undermines and divides the Haudenosaunee people,
against their wishes?*

*The Oneida Nation of New York, Inc., men's council is a new
idea created in 1993 by one person, in defiance of traditional law. In all its
history, the Haudenosaunee never had a governing entity called a "men's
council." Our Iroquois people believed in gender equity. This so-called men's
council was never endorsed by the Oneida people but was, amazingly, recognized by the Bureau of Indian Affairs in a very short time after intense
political lobbying by New York state politicians. The Oneida Nation of
New York, Inc., is not recognized by the Haudenosaunee Confederacy and
accounts to no one for its actions.*

*Sovereignty is the right to self-determination by a nation-state
within a defined territory. In the Iroquois way, we believe our sovereignty is
held by the people, not the government, whose officials serve at our pleasure
and are subject to a given set of laws.*

*True freedom, without arbitrary class, racial, religious, or gender
restrictions, was experienced by our people. It was our version of governance—by the people, for the people—that influenced the creators of the
United States. Sadly, some of our people have abused our nation's status by
using our collective rights for short-term material gain. They have created
an artificial class system. These capitalists have copied the worst parts of*

governance

American-style materialism and are now placing our lands, traditions and spirituality at high risk. Despite the new wealth enjoyed by some Native nations, there is no united effort to defend our treaties or to prevent the further loss of our lands, without which sovereignty becomes a hollow word.

Mary and Carrie Dann

When the United States government says, "One nation under God," they don't speak to indigenous populations. It is part of the falsehood under which the United States has lived and continues to live. For more than thirty years, we have been engaged in a battle to protect our homelands, which the Western Shoshones have occupied for at least 10,000 years. The United States government has been trying to take Western Shoshone lands away from us, though they cannot produce a single document to back up their claim that our lands were taken by gradual encroachment and are now public lands. On the other hand, we have the Treaty of Ruby Valley, which granted access and rights of passage to settlers but never relinquished Western Shoshone title to the land. If they took our land by encroachment, where are all those people who encroached? The only people living out here are Indians. What they are now doing is gradually encroaching on our land. That didn't happen one hundred years ago. It is happening now.

In order to try to break our spirit, the Bureau of Land Management has fined us thousands of dollars for refusing to pay grazing fees. This has always been about the land, our right to continue to use and occupy our lands for the benefit of our families and future generations. It has never been about money, or grazing or overgrazing. Then fully armed BLM agents stormed onto our homelands in armored convoys with helicopters overhead to raid our lands and confiscate our horses and cattle. Other northern Nevada ranchers tried to help us, but the agents threatened to arrest anyone who tried to stop them or even walked onto what they described as public lands.

We have repeatedly asked the federal government for Western Shoshone land transfer documents. If our ancestors agreed to give up or sell this land, we would respect that agreement. But the federal agencies have never given us such documents, and through our own knowledge of Shoshone history, we know that there was never an agreement or document signed by the Western Shoshone that gave away our land. The Inter-American Commission on Human Rights has publicly released a report finding that the U.S. government is violating international human rights' laws in regard to the way it has treated us and our land claims. How can a country that professes to value democracy and human rights act like this? It is morally and ethically wrong.

Joy Harjo

Sovereignty is a state of mind, or I should say, a state of heart. It has more to do with how we conduct daily mundane actions than the heroic acts of war. Do we speak to our children in our Native languages? What name leads us to the Sacred? What rituals do we use to acknowledge our presence here? Tribal sovereignty means the ability to say who you are and what you are and to think for yourself. It means the ability to run your own schools and to move about in the world with dignity, as your own nation.

Jaune Quick-to-See Smith

Nation to nation becomes rhetoric. Truth be known, we live under a colonialist system of government and are controlled by the dominant culture, which is Euro-American.

Still our treaties are the only thing standing between us and oblivion (in the government's eyes). We must constantly stand vigilant. It takes extensive knowledge of Indian law to maneuver through the federal government and courts. We Flatheads have fifty-one full-time lawyers who are primarily protecting our Hellgate Treaty.

The government operates with a not-so-hidden planned obsolescence agenda—that is, to get rid of the American Indian Problem (an ongoing

governance

federal program exactly entitled that way). Here's a quick and dirty run of U.S. history in plain English:

> *Indian people were murdered, exterminated, and left to starve*
>
> *Pushed out of their homes*
>
> *Pushed off their homelands*
>
> *Marched at gunpoint for thousands of miles*
>
> *Given the world's first germ warfare*
>
> *Given new land in exchange for lost land and lives, which changed into small allotments so that the rest of the land could be opened to white homesteaders*
>
> *Given an Indian ID number or Certificate of Degree of Indian Blood with blood quantum listed*
>
> *Separated our children from their parents by turning them over to Christian churches*
>
> *Forbade our people to speak traditional languages or practice traditional religions*
>
> *Sent hundreds away from homelands and dumped them in large cities on relocation plans to separate them from their communities*
>
> *Sterilized women and sent children to welfare homes*

What is it so hard for our history books to recite that? The answer is that our country teaches a whitewashed version of U.S. history to cover their dirty tracks. Recently I made an explanatory drawing called "Indian Affairs Chart." Listed were the U.S. government, the U.S. Supreme Court, the Bureau of Indian Affairs, the federal courts, and a singular title—The Tribes—to enlighten the viewer. I spent considerable time making a mass of black crosshatched lines, which created an impossible-to-read diagram. Most Native people who try to explain our relationship with the government to a white American have the experience of watching them sink from view as they succumb to narcolepsy.

Sarah James

Sovereignty is an inherent right given to us by the Creator when he put us in a certain part of the world to take care of the land in a respectful way for future generations. That is our right and responsibility. We have our own area we consider our traditional land. This land is given to us by the Creator. We didn't come from anywhere else, and we are not going anywhere. Our sovereign right to govern ourselves is not being respected by the federal government. We have taken our human rights' issues to the United Nations, but we only have status as observers there.

Almost two decades ago, our Gwich'in people experienced a revitalization of our nation when our tribal leaders traveled from village to village to discuss our problems and learned that before contact with Europeans, our leaders gathered when our nation was threatened. In keeping with our traditional ways, they called a big meeting of all the villages in June 1988, and the group chose four subjects to discuss: international boundary problems, concerns about caribou, keeping our tribal language, and alcohol and drug abuse.

After three days, the chiefs realized that history was being made. The rebirth of our nation was occurring, and they wanted the world to know about it. They asked the elders if they could pass a resolution to put this history on paper. The resolution was to protect the porcupine caribou calving ground where between 30,000 and 40,000 calves are born each year. We call the birthplace of the porcupine caribou "The Sacred Place Where Life Begins." We are caribou people. That is who we are and how we survived for thousands of years. And now, the caribou were bringing fifteen villages between the North Yukon and northeast Alaska back together again to take a position against oil and gas development. It was the first time we had met in unity like that for more than 150 years. Since that first meeting in 1988, we have remained united on the issue of protecting the coastal plain bordering the Arctic Ocean, which is home to polar bears, extremely rare birds, musk ox, and the birthing grounds of the caribou.

governance

At that meeting in 1988, not that many outsiders knew about us. There was a lot of discussion about the consequences of taking a position against oil and gas development, including a lot of public interest and new threats to our way of life. But in the end, the elders gathered around the campfire and wrote a resolution to protect to coastal plains. They chose four advocates from Canada and four from the United States to make the resolution work. I had the honor of being chosen one of the advocates. They formed this committee on a spiritual foundation. It was a wonderful reunion and renewal of relationships, and there were a lot of prayers and singing. As advocates chosen at that meeting, we were expected to serve for the rest of our lives, unless we chose to step down. The elders instructed us to teach the world in a good way about our people and the land, with one voice, and no compromise. They said, "Outside people don't know who we are, and they need to be taught."

Since that time I have spent most of my time working to protect the coastal plains of the Arctic National Wildlife Refuge and the porcupine caribou calving grounds from oil and gas development. We call the area Porcupine because it crosses the Porcupine River. This area is also where many other life-forms begin. This area is essential for our way of life because we are caribou people. This is a very sacred place for us, and it has not yet been disturbed and should never be disturbed. I have testified before Congress; appeared in print media and on television; spoken to high schools, colleges, and at conferences. With the prayers and help of many people from all over the world, we have been able to protect our land. That is what sovereignty is about.

Audrey Shenandoah

Our nation is divided into clans. My clan is called the Mud House People. Each clan belongs to a certain house. In times of ceremony, people from each side of the clans must have people working together. In times of sickness or death when the family needs help, the opposite clans have the *duty to come and do for those who experience hardship. Because of my age, I seldom do it anymore, but I do delegate different people to go to that house and see what needs to be done. Opposite houses work for one another. The Six Nations Confederacy meetings are held in the longhouse and community meetings are held there as well.*

Many people don't understand the word sovereignty. *Sovereignty is the ability to carry out your own direction. If you think sovereign, you can be sovereign. People use the word all the time, but I don't think they know what it means to act sovereign. Part of sovereignty is being able to see the things you know are right and fight for them.*

Octaviana Valenzuela Trujillo

To my knowledge, I was the first university professor to be elected to a tribal council. I was called to duty by my Pascua Yaqui elders during my first year as a faculty member at the University of Arizona. This to me was a great honor. I accepted the duty even though I knew it could jeopardize my career. Crossing the bridge from academia to nation-building was my greatest challenge and most fulfilling experience to date.

Sovereignty in an indigenous context implies self-reliance, independence, and self-determination. Autonomy seems to be the common ground we indigenous people seek for our contemporary societies.

Angela Gonzales

We use the term consensus *to describe tribal decision making. In my tribal council, decisions are made, but it is certainly not a consensual process. There is serious fighting going on. But people are willing to compromise, and when all the fighting is done, decisions are made and there is a sense that the decision is right for us as a people. At Hopi, tourism is huge. I personally despise tourism. When I visit people, and they learn I am Hopi,*

governance

they want to show me their pottery or maybe a kachina that has vinyl objects and little feathers glued on it. Yet I am very aware of the fact that a cottage industry at home relies on the tourist season to put food on the table.

Rosalie Little Thunder

I think of nationhood and sovereignty in different ways. Nation-hood is a collective consciousness, history, and a sense of responsibility to each other as a functional unit. In a tribal nation, we function independently but never lose the sense of interdependence either. In the past, I don't think we had the collective ego we now have. The term sovereignty *is overused as a shield for lack of responsibility. We maintain the right to govern ourselves, and I dislike paternalism just as much as the next Lakota person, but sov-ereignty demands a lot of responsibility that we are not handling as well as we should. If we are truly sovereign, then we should be able to feed ourselves, and we should maintain our tribal lands in a responsible manner. We're not there yet.*

Some of our tribal governments are driven by self-serving politi-cians, and we can't seem to vote them out of office. If the traditional people were the critical mass, only then would we experience true sovereignty. That is a long process that hasn't even begun, but I have faith that something will happen that will bring the best people in our culture into leadership positions with our governments. Most of our best leaders are defending the land, wildlife, sacred sites, and protecting our lifeways. To these people, leadership is not about self. They are truly selfless people.

womanhood

Chapter Five

I am defined by my will to live.
—Jaune Quick-to-See Smith, Salish Flathead

When asked what it means to be an indigenous woman in the twenty-first century, most of the women at this gathering expressed more interest in discussing what it means to be a good *human being*. They speak of their womanhood within the context of the family, community, and nation. The daily lives of tradition-oriented indigenous women vary greatly, but most express a deep sense of responsibility for the cultural survival of their people. They define what it means to be a woman as they conduct their work and live their lives surrounded by a chaotic, materialistic culture that tries to narrowly define the roles of women. Like women everywhere, indigenous women do not want others defining for them what it means to be a woman.

Though there are many powerful indigenous women, such as Karen Artichoker, Sharon Asetoyer, and Cecilia Fire Thunder, who work on core gender issues such as family violence, pay equity, and reproductive rights, few describe themselves as feminists. They characterize their work as human rights' work. It is work for family, community, and nation. LaDonna Harris, who helped found the National Women's Political Caucus, is one of the few very prominent indigenous women who has been active in the national Women's Rights movement, and I am one of the few elected tribal leaders to consistently describe myself as a feminist. Feminist historian Sally Roesch Wagner points out that the terminology of women's rights may be viewed quite differently by the Haudenosaunee, who see many of these rights as simply their way of living. That could be the case in other communities as well.

Ms. Roesch Wagner has documented the degree to which gender equity in the political and social system of the Haudenosaunee influenced nineteenth-century feminists Elizabeth Cady Stanton, Lucretia Mott, and Matilda Joslyn Gage. Roesch Wagner argues that these three feminists "looked to the Iroquois for their vision of a transformed society." Lucretia Mott spent a month with the Seneca just prior to the 1848 Women's Rights Conference in Seneca Falls. Wagner asks the provocative question, "Where else would feminists of that time find practical examples of gender equity?" Where indeed? Among Euro-Americans, where married women could be legally battered and raped by their spouses? In Europe, where women had little control over their own bodies and few legal rights? Wagner argues persuasively that Stanton and Gage looked at the respect with which Haudenosaunee women were treated and "the everyday decency, nonviolence, and gender justice must have seemed the Promised Land." That everyday decency included only rare instances of physical or sexual assault against women.

Outsiders may not always understand the nuance and complexity of relationships between men and women who are living within a fragmented but still present sense of gender balance. At a recent gathering of indigenous women, Osage activist and artist Anita Fields asked an Osage relative, Andrew Gray, with whom she had a lifelong, trusting relationship, to offer greetings on her behalf to the all-female group. In Osage kinship terms, he is considered her brother. Because Anita gave Andrew the honor of speaking for her, he had to listen very closely to her, learn what was in her heart and mind, and then assume responsibility for speaking from a woman's perspective. Indeed, when Andrew spoke, his thoughts and words were expressed beautifully, reflecting a female sensibility. Anita and Andrew were working from an easy assumption of gender balance and mutual respect that could easily have been misinterpreted by outsiders.

Rosalie Little Thunder describes a time when she returned to the reservation and was not completely sure of the protocol for making a presentation to the tribal council. Her cousin offered to present her issue to the council and to act as a buffer and spokesperson, an offer Rosalie readily accepted. No rational person who knows Rosalie Little Thunder would describe her as subservient to men or to anyone.

Lurline Wailana McGregor explains that women in other indigenous cultures were also treated with respect, and she notes the irony of having those values systematically destroyed by a society that now wants to help restore them: "The Western concept of women's liberation is just meaningless to me. We didn't need all that until outsiders came along and took away all our rights. In ancient times women were not abused like they are now. They had the right to pack up and leave and take everything with them. If they were so inclined, women could become warriors and fight along with the men. Now, the women's rights people want us to fight for equality in their context: equal pay and more steps up the corporate ladder. There is nothing wrong with that kind of power, but it is not going to equalize us."

Octaviana Valenzuela Trujillo acknowledges she has benefited from the Women's Rights and Civil Rights movements but questions the relevance of mainstream feminism to some indigenous women. She characterizes mainstream feminism as the "struggle to be recognized primarily as an individual and not as a member of a gender class. This has multiple implications for all women, as well as special implications for indigenous women who consider the traditional values of indigenous cultures paramount to the self-determination of the individual."

Audrey Shenandoah adds, "Balance between men and women is

womanhood

very important. A lot of people have the misconception that women in our communities were and are more important than men. That is not so. The power of women is recognized and utilized. Women have always had the responsibility and privilege of choosing the leadership among our people, a practice that continues even today. Once the leadership is chosen, the Clan Mother and the leader must consult with one another and work closely together. Neither has more power than the other. When the chiefs sit in council, the women are present, and when they have a difficult decision to make, they always call on the women for their opinion."

Astonished at the absence of women in delegations of colonial negotiators in the eighteenth century, one of our Cherokee chiefs asked, "Where are your women?" As we move confidently forward into the twenty-first century, we must all ask that question again and again until the truthful answer can be "women are everywhere they want to be."

Wilma Mankiller

My Great-Aunt Maggie Gourd was a very good storyteller who believed in the power of dreams. She once told us about a dream in which a large animal—a bull or a buffalo—tried to break into her house by repeatedly ramming her front door. When she woke up the next morning, her front door was badly damaged. I remember only tiny fragments of the dream stories Maggie shared, but I recall clearly that in her stories, there were no absolute lines between dreams and reality. Maggie also told us stories about Little People, *Yunwi Tsunsdi*, who live in rocky places like a bluff near freshwater wherever Cherokees reside. They are only about three feet tall. They sing and speak in Cherokee. ... Cherokee people describe Little People as "secondhand." It is often said that if one sees the Little People and tells about it, that person will soon die.

My mother-in-law, the late Florence Soap, told me that her father used to gather medicine for her sister from a certain place.

Then one day, for the first time, he took her to a new place to look for medicine. When her sister asked him why they couldn't go back to the old place, he said the Little People told him not to come back to gather medicine there. He soon got sick and died. Florence said, "If he hadn't told my sister about seeing the Little People, he would probably have lived longer. That's what we believe." Also, if anything out of the ordinary is found in the woods, Cherokees assume that it belongs to the Little People. If a Cherokee woman goes out to gather hickory nuts and happens on a woven basket left by another gatherer, she can pick it up and say out loud, "Little People, I am taking this basket." Then it is hers to keep. That is her right.

There were other important women in my early childhood but none more important than my mother, Irene Sitton Mankiller, who has provided me with a lifetime of unconditional love. My mother worked alongside my other siblings and my father on income-producing projects as well as the dozens of daily chores required to keep a large family fed and cared for. My mother never sat me down and said this is how you should live or this is what it means to be a woman. I learned a lot from watching her and the other women around me. I remain grateful to both my parents for never telling me, "Girls can't do that," and for letting me define for myself what it means to be a woman.

Then there were the "bless-your-little-heart" ladies. They were white Christian women who made our family one of their charities by bringing used clothing and other gifts to our small wood frame home. When I saw their big car approaching our house, I ran and hid. While walking to and from school, they would sometimes stop and offer us a ride, murmuring, "Bless your little hearts." Even at a very early age, I understood that these women thought they were better than us and that they would accept us if only we were more like them. Many years later, a white woman raising money to give college scholarships to indigenous students told me she wanted to "give pride back to the Indians." She had such a staggering sense of entitlement; she didn't know the highly insulting and patronizing nature of that

womanhood

statement. She reminded me of the "bless-your-little-heart" ladies from my childhood.

After we made the wrenching move to California, a number of women reached out to me. Without them, I don't know how I could ever have become a successful adult. I especially value the time I had with my maternal grandmother, Pearl Sitton, who was a reassuring presence during a time when I felt confused, lost, and out of place in San Francisco. In school I was teased a lot and labeled as different because I had an unusual last name, spoke with an Oklahoma accent, and looked "ethnic." But the biggest differences stemmed from the very divergent life experiences of the other children and me. While they had learned to ride a bicycle, skate on roller skates, or play with the hula hoop, I had never even spoken on a telephone or used a flush commode before our arrival in San Francisco.

During my adolescence, I spent most summers with Grandma Sitton and lived with her for a year while attending the eighth grade at Lone Tree School in nearby Escalon, California. Grandma Sitton was an extremely independent and affectionate woman who had moved to California to start over again after the death of my grandfather. She liked to sing gospel songs as she worked in the house or in the garden. She was a disciplined woman who was up before sunrise each morning and in bed shortly after nightfall. It was clear where my mother got her work values.

Several single mothers at the San Francisco Indian Center made quite an impression on me as well. They held clerical or professional jobs, did volunteer work at the Indian center, and helped each other. My sister and I watched their children while they went dancing in the ballroom of the San Francisco Indian Center or some other fun place. On Saturday night, they gathered at Justine Buckskin's house to joke and tease each other as they got ready for their big night out. I loved watching the women work their hair into impossibly high hairdos, glue it together with Aqua Net hair spray, and then teeter out the front door on high heels, assuring us they would be back by midnight, a goal they never met. To a twelve-year-old, their lives seemed full and exciting. Much later I learned that they found their beautiful Saturday night outfits in the clothing bins at Saint Vincent de Paul's thrift shop on Fourteenth and Mission Streets, and that they often struggled to make ends meet, relying on one another to get from one payday to the next. Though they adjusted to life in the city, they longed to return to their tribal communities, and most eventually did. These women were resourceful, doing the best they could with what they had and taking the time to find joy in their families, friendships, and their special nights out. Even today the heavy scent of Aqua Net hair spray makes me smile and remember those resilient women.

Like my counterparts at the Indian center, a beehive hairdo was perched precariously on my head when I was married just a few days before my eighteenth birthday in November of 1963. My husband expected me to step completely away from involvement in the Indian center and from my birth family. It was a tall order. I had an avid interest in social justice issues and the extraordinary world around me. At that time in San Francisco, there were many debates and discussions of Red Power, civil rights, and women's rights. Musicians Janis Joplin and Jimi Hendrix were introducing a completely new sound to a generation now known as baby boomers, and the Haight-Ashbury district was becoming a mecca for middle-class young people. There was a free-speech movement at the University of California at Berkeley and massive anti-war demonstrations throughout the Bay Area. By the time I was twenty-three, any notion that I could live my life as a wife and mother as defined by my husband and the social constraints of that time was gone forever. I became involved in the community, started thinking about attending college, and the beehive hairdo, makeup, and heels were replaced by long straight hair and sensible shoes.

In 1976 when my daughters, Felicia and Gina, and I returned to Oklahoma, I was more independent, self-confident, and had acquired some knowledge of land and treaty rights as well as grant-writing skills. I also had an abiding faith in the ability of Cherokee

womanhood

people to solve their own problems, and I immediately began developing community-based programs that reflected that philosophy.

At that time, there were no female executives with the Cherokee Nation—and there had never been a female deputy chief or principal chief. In historic times, women played an important role in Cherokee government and in tribal life, but that role had diminished over time. As Cherokee people began to intermarry with whites and adopt the values of the larger society, women increasingly assumed a secondary role. When I first ran for election as deputy principal chief in 1983, it seemed the strong role of women in Cherokee life had been forgotten by some of our own people. I vividly remember a man standing up in a campaign meeting and telling me, "Cherokee Nation will be the laughingstock of all the tribes if we elect a woman." Though there was considerable opposition to my candidacy, I was elected to serve a four-year term as the first female deputy principal chief in Cherokee history. I thought this was my summit in tribal government, but I was elected to serve as principal chief in 1987—the first woman to hold that position—and resoundingly reelected again in 1991.

By the time I left office in 1995, after not seeking a fourth four-year term of office, there were fewer questions about whether or not women should be in leadership positions in the Cherokee Nation. If people opposed me, it was because they disagreed with my policies, not just because I am female. Cherokee people are more concerned about competency—about whether the Head Start bus shows up on time or whether they are properly diagnosed at the health clinics—than whether a woman is leading the nation. In a way, my elections were a step forward for women and a step into the Cherokee tradition of balance between men and women.

every day is a good day

The Gathering
Mary and Carrie Dann

Western Shoshone women are taught that a woman is like the Earth: she gives and nurtures life. The Earth and women have the same properties. The Earth provides for us, just as we provide for our children. The way we were taught, if the Earth is treated with disrespect by a woman, she is disrespecting herself. We are one and the same.

Indigenous women are going to have to fight for the rights of the Earth, but other races of women should not just stand aside and let the body of the Earth be destroyed. They are allowing the destruction of their own body. When women see nuclear destruction and storage, they should make every attempt to put a stop to it. All living things are the Earth's children.

In the future, women will have to watch their children, grandchildren, and great-grandchildren suffer from the damage being done by the governments of the world. Most people in power are men. They are irresponsible. When they rape the Earth, they are raping us as well. Physical rape comes to women because men have no respect for the female spirit. Before the coming of the white people, one didn't hear about men violating women. The violation came during the time of the white settlers—the Spanish and the English.

There are some exceptions, but most of our men's minds have been colonized, and they have suffered. Also, everything is sexualized. It is really frightening. Almost every advertisement includes some sex, and then people wonder why women are violated. Now it is to the point where it is no longer good enough to violate our women, they want to violate boys and girls. Things are way off balance.

When we were little, grandmother would sit at the table and talk almost every day, and we would listen. She told special stories in the wintertime, and a lot of Creation stories. She also spoke with us about what human beings should do and the role of all living things. My aunt and mother also played an important role in our lives and shaped who we are. The fact that we did not go away to an Indian boarding school was

womanhood

important. We went to public schools, therefore we weren't forced to attend church. We were brought up with traditional beliefs.

Audrey Shenandoah

The role of women is very complex and important. Many women have begun to lose a sense of self-esteem, of their importance to the human race and to this Earth. Women have to understand the role of being a very special person and the importance of being able to carry life, to give life, and to nurture it from the beginning. In our way, women are free to pursue whatever they are capable of doing, except the activities that harm the internal organs or interfere with childbearing, such as playing lacrosse. Our women do not play lacrosse because they develop muscles that create diffi- culty in birthing. In our traditions, we are told that a long time ago, younger women always had their own lodge where they could go when they were on their moon (menstrual cycle).

Using the Moon as a guide, the women discuss and decide when the ceremonies will be held. At one time the Faith Keepers watched the Moon activity very closely and made decisions based totally on the Moon. Our lives are now so interwoven with the larger society that we plan the ceremonies by the calendar. With so many people working, we schedule our ceremonies on weekends. Women have the duty of planning and preparing medicine and food for the ceremonies, even though the men actually perform the ceremonies. Women have their own ceremonies, in which men help with the singing and giveaways (honoring gifts). The men have one very strong ceremony where they handle everything. If a woman is involved, it will be a woman who no longer has a menstrual cycle because of the power that women have during that time. The power can affect the medicine in many ways, including spoiling it or making it go bad. Balance is important in everything we do. When the Women's Rights movement began, they asked women from our communities to speak because they thought we were more powerful than the men, that we made all the decisions for our people. Some of them are still trying to make themselves not only equal but superior to men, without any recognition that there should be balance.

The Clan Mothers, the grandmothers, the aunts, and the elders were the ones who had the honor and responsibility of nurturing young minds of the children. When a baby is born, the Clan Mothers give them their name. The way we describe it in our language is that the Clan Mothers have a bag of names by them and when a baby is born, they reach in the bag and choose a name for the baby. From the time of birth until children were about seven years of age, they were entrusted to the women. They weren't isolated from the rest of the settlement, but the young children spent most of their time with the women who were responsible for nurturing these little spirits. They taught the children how to take care of one another. They taught them survival skills, how to gather medicine, and how to determine what was good and bad for them. Then after the special time with the women, the children were mixed with the rest of society where their talents were recognized—one may have the gift of singing, another the gift of dancing or being a good speaker. Nurturing the mind and body were the most important things in our people's history.

In English the process for helping children develop their unique talents would be described as tutorship. When the boys were ten or eleven, they were given responsibility and were taught more things that require travel, endurance, and physical ability. The girls knew where to fish for different kinds of fish or where the seasonal berries were located. They learned these things just from being with the elders, seeing how things were done, and seeing how to be content with their lives. And they were always happy. Our people were full of laughter. There was nothing to be unhappy about. No one sat them down and taught them.

We learn everything from our grandmothers. They didn't sit us down with a book or paper and say, "Now you write this down and remember this." We learned from hearing what was important in our lives over and over again. Even if young people say they have heard it all before, we have to keep repeating things that build their character. I can remember my grandmother saying in our own language, "To my last breath, I will still be telling you

womanhood

these things." Maybe young people sometimes don't want to listen, but the only way to perpetuate the knowledge is to keep telling them. The nurturing of the mind and body is the most important thing in our people's history.

Gail Small

In the Battle of Rosebud, a young woman saw her brother go down on the battlefield. She rode her horse into battle, swooped down and picked up her brother, and escaped. In our tribe we call that "The Battle Where the Girl Saved Her Brother." She was a very powerful warrior woman in our tribe. We believe that her blood is in our veins and that we carry that blood with a strong heart into struggles.

Our identity as Indian women is very grounded in the land. We can't separate ourselves from that. And we're born into this struggle for the land. I've never really had a choice of going out and being some wealthy corporate lawyer. I knew I was going to be fighting for my land, because that's all we have ever known. A long time ago, there was a clear understanding of the responsibilities between men and women. Men and women knew they needed each other's help to get things done. There was give and take in the relationships. Even in ceremonial life, the Sun Dance cannot go on without the women, though they do not actually do the Sun Dance.

The relationship between Cheyenne men and women varies by generation. We now have a lot of adult men in leadership who were emotionally crippled by their boarding school experience. Some exhibit very angry behavior and have difficulty maintaining respectful relationships with women. Also, some of my Cheyenne people have a history of serving in the military. The men who served in Vietnam were really affected by that experience and struggle with a lot of issues. The older generations that were not confined to boarding schools are very loving. My dad's generation gives tremendous love not only to our family but also to every one of our people.

People outside our communities erroneously think tribal people are constrained by expectations of the group. But it is not like that. There is

every day is a good day

tremendous respect for individuality and the freedom to choose what you want to do. Some years ago, when I decided I could no longer continue to serve on the tribal council, the woman who I was named after said, "I heard you are not going to run for tribal council again." When I affirmed that I would not and explained that I was having a hard time being a mother to my four small children and keeping up with all my work, she gave me a big hug and said, "You do what's right. Your children are young for just a short time. Now is when they need you. After your kids grow up, you can go back and do that." Instead of trying to push me to stay in office, a woman who had always played a role in my life affirmed my choice.

Octaviana Valenzuela Trujillo

My mother, Maria, had little formal education and an irresponsible husband, but she persisted in raising eleven sons and daughters against all odds. To maintain order in such a household, she had to promote and employ a strong notion of fairness to all of us in her disciplinary actions, as well as to persevere in doing the "right thing" in her role as a mother and as a woman. For this I admire her. It is because of her that I believe that womanhood personifies justice and persistence. A good woman is fair and has the perseverance of doing the "right thing." Our role as women is seen by many as a disadvantage. In many cases, we are treated as having a handicap, thereby requiring persistence to fulfill our life's goals.

Gender equity is an integral component of traditional Yaqui culture. Yaqui women are part of the warrior society and play a role in selecting the most capable man to lead the village. Although Yaquis in their traditional homelands of northwest Mexico have for the most part continued to observe centuries of traditional governance patterns, Yaquis in the United States have not done so. Unfortunately, the ever-increasing adoption of western European religion and customs by the Yaquis has resulted in an ascendancy of male dominance in their cultural landscape, both in the United States and to a lesser extent, in Mexico. This was evident when I was serving as the vice

womanhood

chair of the Pascua Yaqui Tribe. Our chairman died and I was sworn as the first woman chair of the tribe. The male councilmen, who comprised the majority of the council, specifically and explicitly removed me from office because I am a woman. I had the opportunity to be reinstated through legal channels, but I opted not to pursue this route as I felt at that point and in that context I could provide more effective leadership by working with my council adversaries through collective means rather than confronting them over my position. History has shown the wisdom of that decision as each of my adversaries subsequently apologized for his stance and pledged me unconditional support for any and all further efforts I would take in the name of the Pascua Yaqui.

My personal identity as a woman and a human is very tied to my people. I hope to be remembered as a Yaqui (Yoeme) from the community of Guadalupe who was truly bicultural, bicognitive, and bilingual. If my people speak of me in the distant future, I hope they will say I was a reasonable person and that I was not afraid to challenge injustice. Years from now, if we still have a distinct tribal community amidst the urban sprawl, I want to be remembered as a community leader.

Angela Gonzales

One can be independent and autonomous and still be part of the larger community. It's not an either/or situation. I am adamantly opposed to essentialist notions as to what it means to be a Hopi woman, an Indian woman, a scholar, or an artist. I think there needs to be allowances for our own individual expression. Hopi women are very powerful. The older women are role models that I would like to emulate. An elder has a quiet dignity. Have you ever been present when someone quietly enters the room? No loud voice, no flash, no credentials, no symbolism of dress or other smoke screens to conceal oneself? That is how these women are. They have a quiet sense of self. One doesn't have to say what one has accomplished. One doesn't demand respect. Respect is given. In the larger society, you put out your

every day is a good day

curriculum vitae and are defined by your public accomplishments. It is about power and being in the limelight.

At Hopi, the women put so much of themselves into feeding the people, especially during the dances. When we are having tribal dances in the village, all the women come together to support one another and to cook for other families. One of the interesting modern adaptations is that women who are now working outside the home don't have time to make traditional Hopi breads, so a cottage industry has sprung up where some women make the bread and sell it by the box to the women who are too busy to make it themselves. When I was in graduate school in New York, I related to a friend of mine how much I enjoyed going home, and getting there with my twenty-five-pound sack of Blue Bird flour, and making big vats of bread dough. One summer I actually got tendinitis from working the dough so long. My friend from graduate school said, "Oh Angela, you just don't realize the bonds of your own oppression." And I thought that was such an interesting perspective. In Western culture, that is the way it would be perceived. Feminists would come in and ask, "Why are you in this subservient role?"

I have often had trouble with feminists who come into our community and see us working in complementary roles and assume that because we provide food for the people, we are subservient to men. We do these things for the benefit of all. It is an important role to be able to work with other women in a supportive way to provide food for the people. It is a respectful thing. In times past, men and women worked for the benefit of everyone in complementary, balanced relationships. If that means that men sometimes do certain things and women do certain things, it is for the common good.

womanhood

Beatrice Medicine

Our societies are patrilineal in terms of kinship. Males and females work together to keep the family and the kinship nexus intact in order to maintain the nation. The tiospaye *of extended kin is very crucial. The roles of men and women are intertwined. To be a good Lakota woman and for our brothers to be good Lakota men, we have to help each other. Our relationships are very complex. An Indian man once said to me, "Bea, in the old days, women walked ten paces behind a man." And I said, "Oh yes, that's very true. We were telling you where to go." Actually, the warriors were in front and back protecting the people. Warriors shared their knowledge and skills and fought to protect their family, their* tiospaye, *and their nation. Men and women are leaders and I feel very strongly that we must maintain respect and honor between males and females and transmit that to our children.*

There was always balance between men and women but it really changed over time. Some of our men have picked up the patrilineal model and the notion of male superiority. But there are men and women getting together to support each other, seeking to restore the balance.

To be a good Lakota woman, and for our brothers to be good Lakota men, we have to help other people in whatever capacity we can. It is difficult to try to compartmentalize our lives. We have learned to assess the social situation and act accordingly. It is not schizophrenic to discern the proper behavior in different roads of life. As a Lakota woman, I know how to act when I am a professor.

There used to be a very, very important ceremony, the Bite the Knife Society, for elder women who were no longer menstruating. During this ceremony someone put on a feast for a woman who had lived a good life. A knife was put down, and if anyone in the village wanted to tell a story about her, they would touch the knife to indicate truthfulness. But they are not doing that ceremony any more.

every day is a good day

Joanne Shenandoah

Women have the ability to give life, and our Creation story about Sky Woman describes the connection of women to the Earth, the sky, and animals. The elders, such as Alice Papineau and my mother, Maisie Shenandoah (both Clan Mothers), have been the most resolute in protecting our territory and communities. They are strong women who have stood their ground. We heed their counsel while acknowledging their right to have the final say over the nation's decisions.

I come from a long line of strong and proud Native women. My grandmother, Mary Cornelius Winder, and her sister, Delia Waterman, who celebrated her one-hundredth birthday in the year 2000, helped begin the Oneida land claims by writing letters to Washington. My grandmother was a remarkable woman who traveled overseas by ship, had ten children of her own, and as a midwife delivered more than one hundred babies at Onondaga. Early in life I learned that women are in charge, that they make the final decisions about everything. I thought it was that way for everyone. When I went into the corporate world, it was a rude awakening to discover that women are not respected or listened to. Until that time I didn't realize the difficulty most women have in the world.

Joy Harjo

My most positive role model was my Aunt Lois Harjo, on my father's side. She was an artist, a painter who once had a jewelry store. She was a champion of art who gave many hours in support of the collections at the Creek council house in Okmulgee, Oklahoma. She was the one who told me stories, made me realize that my perceptions of crossover between dreaming and this reality weren't crazy. It's difficult to talk of my mother. She didn't know how to mother; she still doesn't know how. For many years, I chose not to deal with her. I had a really hard time with the choices she made for herself because those terrible choices hurt all of us. I have

womanhood

learned to forgive my mother. She did the best she could. I don't think she has forgiven herself.

My mother is Cherokee, Irish, and French. Her mother, my grand-mother, was Cherokee and Irish, and my grandfather was mostly French. My mother grew up in terrible poverty in Arkansas, just across the Oklahoma line. Her mother was raised near there in a full-blood Cherokee community. My mother's mother didn't know how to mother either. She was orphaned and raised by a family who mistreated her. By the time my mother met my father, she had been pretty beaten down by struggle and shame. My father was a very powerful, charismatic, and sexy Creek man. His mother died shortly after he was born, and my father was raised in a chaotic household. His parents sent him off to the Ponca Military Academy.

My mother reveled in romantic love and the idea of being swept away and saved. She was swept away, but wound up in a marriage destroyed by his violence and unfaithfulness. She reluctantly left because to leave meant the destruction of a dream. She almost immediately married a terrorist, and she would not leave because she was worried about starving—a legitimate concern. When I was with my mother, I got buried in her pain; I was always connected to her. I'm convinced the birth cord is long, stays with us through this life. My mother's pain was her mother's pain, and that goes all the way back to North Carolina, before the Cherokees were removed from their homeland. The journey makes an emotional path, worn down over and over again. How do you make a shift? A change? I honor my mother's path now.

Jaune Quick-to-See Smith

I am defined by my will to survive, not by intelligence or cunning or money or good looks. The Creator didn't see her way clear to give me those things, instead she gave me a strong will. Our lives changed forever when my mother (a mixed-blood Cree) left my father (a Flathead, Shoshone, and Metis). My mother dropped me and my sister off at the home of a kindly Indian couple who lived down the road from us. When Daddy came home that night, everything was changed. I became the caretaker for my sister, and

every day is a good day

he became the mother we no longer had, a well as the alcoholic father who was dysfunctional.

If the Great Depression was hard on white folks, it was tenfold harder on Indians. We moved from place to place looking for itinerant work or an occasional horse trade. Sometimes, we had little more than the clothes on our backs, which my dad saw as a plus. He always said, "Sis, it means we can travel light."

We bunked in with other Indian families, especially Salish, because my dad could converse with them. We lived at Hupa, Muckleshoot, Nisqually, and other reservations I can't recall. I do remember Nisqually because we lived with three other families in a one-room cabin. We children rolled up in our blankets against the walls so the grown-ups wouldn't step on us when they came in drunk.

Sometimes a sheriff would take my sister and me away to a foster home where we would get a big, mostly unpleasant dose of white people. But then my dad would sober up and return for us, making new promises of unconditional love and a better future together. He tried. God knows he tried. But the discrimination against dark-skinned men outweighed his ability to cope. He also was a fish out of water. Raised by three or four intergenerational women of tradition, my dad could ride a horse before he could walk, knew all the places to dig camas and bitterroot, knew how to make a decent stew, and knew trading inside and out, which was a tribal enterprise for thousands of years.

When the horses came to the Salish sometime in the late 1700s, we took to them as though joined in body and spirit, men as well as women. We bred the finest stock and treasured our large herds. We were the horse people par excellence and the envy of the northern plains. We were often raided by the Blackfeet, Crow, and Sioux, who were all being squeezed out of the homelands and were driven ragged by the white invaders.

Maybe that imprint on our DNA gave my dad, my sister, and me some tenacity, some will to survive. When I turned six, my dad showed up one last time at a welfare home with a white woman in tow and announced that she was the long-lost mother we had been looking for. Hogwash was a

womanhood

word that went round in my head, but I played along.

 From my white stepmother, Mertice, I learned how I didn't want to behave or think or live. She was impatient, demanding, whipped us with tree switches, and was stingy with Indians, never wanting to feed them when they came by. I only wanted to imitate my father's kindness, patience, good heart, generosity, and way with a horse.

 My father was raised by one of my grandmothers, who was purchased for $50 by a French trader, which was the custom for many Indian women in the late 1800s. They were pack animals and slaves for the traders. Another grandmother who helped raise my father went out to round up the cattle one morning and had a heart attack, fell off her horse, and died—with her boots on, you could say. My belief is that my father transferred some of the goodness and strength of these women to me by osmosis—at least I want to believe that.

 My father never told me to be a little lady; he only told me where to stand while he drove thundering herds of horses at me in a roundup. He never told me to "think pink" but he did make me help build corrals and chop wood. When I turned eight years old, he sent me out to work permanently. After school, on weekends, and in the summers I worked for the Nisei (Japanese Americans) when they returned from the internment camps. It wasn't for money he said, although we needed it, but to help build my character. All in all, this must have helped me locate that will to survive, the one that defines who I am.

Faith Smith

 It is important to develop and feel comfortable with a uniquely Native female kind of leadership instead of one modeled after white males— or white females, for that matter. We need to feel comfortable with what works for us, not feel embarrassed by it, or feel it is less important than other styles of leadership. Women build more bridges and try to find connections instead of confrontation. Women have to negotiate all the time, from the moment we get up until we go to bed at night. We may not like everybody, but we can build a long-term agenda without camps or factions.

I had amazing female role models from the time I started school. When I began working at the Chicago Indian Center, the women leaders were very strong. They had raised their children and worked full-time. They rolled up their sleeves and made a positive place for their family and their community. Most of these women could have worked any place in the world, but they chose to work in the community. Work in the community is hard. You don't get strokes from within your own community.

Linda Aranaydo

During the occupation of Alcatraz Island I learned a lot about being a woman in a community. From my grandparents and mother, I always knew who I was, but there was no community surrounding me to help me make decisions as I wondered, "How am I going to be? What kind of woman am I going to grow into if I haven't been around a lot of women?" The friend-ships I made at Alcatraz have lasted now for more than thirty-five years, and I expect them to last a lifetime. When we occupied Alcatraz I was a senior in college. I finished my degree requirements at U.C. Berkeley by commuting twice a week back and forth from the island to the mainland.

As long as I can remember I have been interested in social justice issues. In 1968 I joined Martin Luther King's Poor People's March, and then in 1969, along with thirteen other students, we occupied Alcatraz Island. Fourteen of us went to Fisherman's Wharf and got on a boat to Alcatraz. In my twenty-year-old mind, it seemed like a logical response to the fact that the San Francisco Indian Center had burned down and we really no longer had a place to gather. We were completely unprepared for what we found on the island. We started running around, hiding from the caretaker and his dog. Some of the guys were Vietnam veterans, and I thought they would know how to lead us. We broke up into small groups and hid overnight. The next day, the Coast Guard came and negotiated our

womanhood

removal. *The following morning, the Coast Guard removed us and dropped us off at Fisherman's Wharf. So, we decided to just eat some French bread and crab and think about what to do next. One minute we were breaking all kinds of federal laws, and the next we were pooling our money for French bread and crab cocktail.*

The second time we occupied the island, we planned it and we knew a little more. I understood there may be consequences for participating in the occupation of federal land, but it seemed like the right thing to do at the time. At that time, the outside world defined us as the poorest of the poor, the unhealthiest of the unhealthy, and everything that was written about us began with the phrase "the plight of the American Indian." We didn't feel like we were in the middle of a plight, we felt like we were in the middle of our lives. We were young and wanted to see changes, to see what we could do at Alcatraz. Two years later, when the occupation was over, I was teaching school in an Oakland neighborhood where lots of the families of those who had occupied Alcatraz had settled. Four years later we had our own Indian preschool for our kids. I then had my two sons, Nathan and Alec. I learned to cook and teach and raise kids and make community with my family and their families. The preschool grew into the Hintil KuuCa Children's Center for preschoolers and after-school care. I will always know families from this time in my life. As a group of intertribal young families, we wanted to raise our children to know who they were even if we lived in the city. When they were older, my children would go to the Stanford Powwow and look for their friends from Hintil, their "Oakland tribe" of Navajo, Sioux, Pomo, Paiute, Miwok, Wintun, Chippewa, Creek, Pima, and Papago friends. While working as a physician in northern California clinics, I have been delighted to do a preschool physical exam on the child of one of my former students.

I continue to work to relieve the physical causes of pain as I learn more about meditation and mindfulness. I am very interested in how we create some of our own suffering in the processes of our mind. I'm grateful for a life that offers me, a Muscogee Creek born so far from home, the opportunity to dance in the spiral at Hillabee Stomp Dance grounds with my relatives and feel at peace.

every day is a good day

Lurline Wailana McGregor

*When you look around the Hawaiian community today, it is clear
that there are more women in leadership positions than men. There needs
to be more balance between the two for the health of the community, which
means finding a way to reempower men.*

*I think colonization was much harder on men than on women
because there was more pressure on men to assimilate into the Western
culture. The land was crucial to the daily life of traditional society. It provided
everything we needed, including the ability to exchange goods with other
members of the community, such as fish for taro, or access to the forests
to build canoes. When foreigners came in and took the land for their own
economic purposes and prevented Hawaiians from having access to it, there
was often no choice but to move to town and integrate into Western society
in order to survive and provide for your family. Not unlike other indigenous
communities that have undergone similar colonization, the results have been
high rates of alcoholism, drug abuse, domestic violence, welfare dependency,
and so on. We are struggling with that now, and sometimes it seems there is
no end in sight. The dysfunction has become generational, and that makes it
much more difficult to overcome.*

Rosalie Little Thunder

*As a matriarch, I think I could write an entire book on the chal-
lenges and responsibilities of womanhood. We are the creators of "home,"
caretakers of the spiritual and physical needs of the* tiwahe, *or household,
and our* tiospaye, *or extended family. We are teachers, healers, storytellers,
peacemakers, problem solvers, and visionaries. The roles and responsibilities
in indigenous cultures are different and dynamic. Unless humanity evolves
to a point where we are all asexual, I don't think we will get true equity,
whatever that is. I am not sure we should wish for that. Feminism is a Euro-
American response to a misogynist problem created by Euro-Americans.*

womanhood

My experience as a Lakota has been that women are the center of male existence. We are matriarchal, not because someone made a conscious decision that this was to be the case. Our ways evolved out of need, in a natural way, according to natural law. My grandfather, my father, and my brothers respected and were all concerned for me as a female child. I had the final word, and I learned to be careful with my influence. I am now the matriarch of my growing tiospaye, or extended family unit.

Outside observers filter our experience through their own lens and may focus on an isolated situation and then determine we are subservient to men. Men's historical role was to provide and protect, but the reservation period stripped them of the very need for their existence. The male role was severely damaged when families were confined and fed rations, and children were sent to boarding schools. When male leaders went to prison, their response was deep loss and anger. The women's role remained intact and therefore, we survived well. So when our leadership was in demand again, we were there.

Sarah James

Women and men once had the same roles in our society because we were nomadic people who lived in vast, harshly cold, open areas. If a woman had to wait for her husband to come back to bring in some food from the hunt or chop the wood or keep the home warm, she would not survive. Women had to know how to survive. The men had to know how to cook when they were out somewhere. The dress for the women and the men was almost identical. They both wore pants, but the shirttail for the men was a bit longer, and women had a hood for a baby carrier—but some men also had hoods and carried babies. Women did not wear dresses. It would be very difficult to walk in the deep snow wearing a dress and snowshoes. Some women who had the time did make dresses for traditional dances only. Now it seems that society expects different roles from men and women, and that is kind of confusing.

My mother taught me that the ability to give birth gives women a

every day is a good day

lot of power. We are to use that power in a good way. She taught me that men are vulnerable and can be easily taken advantage of, and that we should be respectful toward them and not overpower them.

I grew up traditionally, speaking the Gwich'in language and following the caribou migration. From both my parents and my grandparents, I learned that womanhood means being respectful toward others and being willing to work, not expecting others to do everything for you. When I was chosen by my people to speak out to protect our lands, they did not talk about my being a woman. They chose me as one of the people they thought could do the job best. They expected results from my work as an advocate for the Arctic National Wildlife Refuge and the birthplace of the porcupine caribou, not as a woman.

Florence Soap

My mother taught me how to be a woman. She kept a beautiful garden with beans, corn, potatoes, yams, tomatoes, cucumbers, lettuce, and mustard. We canned everything we ate back then. We made hominy out of the corn, and we ground our own cornmeal. We made our own flour with wheat. We were able to store potatoes through even the coldest winter weather by lining the potatoes on hay and then covering them in hay. We made big barrels of sauerkraut. We ate squirrel, rabbit, fish, and hog meat, which we dried, preserved with salt, and stored in our smokehouse. When we were children, we would all go hunting for rabbit. When it snowed, we would wrap our feet in (burlap) and go out and hunt rabbit. At night we would find robins and use a flashlight to startle them, then hit them on the head. The elders would stay up late cleaning the robins or rabbits we brought home. There was no separation between the boys and the girls. The boys helped out with the household chores and the girls went out to hunt, even in the snow. We very rarely had free time, but when we did have a little time to ourselves, the girls and boys played marbles, hide-and-go-seek, or other games we made up from our own imagination.

We lived in a log house with no windows. During the day in the

womanhood

wintertime, we never closed the door so we would have light in the cabin. We only had one room with a stove, a table for our meals, and shelves to store things. Mom and Dad had a bed, but the children all slept on a blanket on the floor. We had a lot of chores: hoeing cotton and corn, cutting and gathering wood, pulling weeds, or doing other work. During the summer, we would hunt huckleberries all day long. We could sell the berries for twenty-five cents a gallon in town. We would use the money to buy salt or coffee. This practical knowledge and ability to make do with what I had was very helpful to me as an adult.

Dr. Beatrice Medicine, *on the passing of her mother*

Ina

Nameless one—
Hastily called "Butte Woman"
Paha win
By the keeper of the
White Buffalo Calf Woman's Pipe

A woman of many names,
All kinship designations—
Tuwin—*aunt*
Oonchi—*grandmother*
Cuwe—*older sister*
Hankashi—*female cousin*
Ina—*mother*
All honorable,
All good.

I prefer
Napewakanwin
"Sacred Hands Woman"
Suggested by our own wapiya
The healer.
But refused by you
As being too honoring.

The wapiya *now insists*
That you were given the name
Wapahaluta win
"RedWarbonnet Woman"
when you were a child.

But nameless one, in Lakota,
Your deeds live on and are
Recounted.

I knew that you would remain
For Christmas—a Christian celebration
A time you enjoyed,
A festivity,
A ritual.
"The more the merrier,"
You always said
About the houseful of tiospaye *members.*
An extended family of drunks,
Free-loaders,
Homeless ones,
Arrogant ones,
Lazy ones.

womanhood

January was a worry for me, too.
It must have been for you.
You often said,
"If I make it through January … "
Moon of Cracking Limbs,
Of trees,
Of people,
Of thoughts.

But you called this moon
"When the door is blocked."
Snow, fine and dry,
Blowing, swirling, stacking
Against the tipi flap,
Now the wooden door
Of the log cabin.

I recall your concern for others.
"I'd rather not die
in winter time …
It's too hard
For the grave-diggers."

I knew
It would be more rewarding
To start the final journey
Atop a scaffold—looking upward
Toward the "spirit trail"
The Milky Way

The "Spirit Trail"
Is bright and smoothly shining
In the "moon of Black Cherries"
Of
"When the Tree Limbs Crack."

It seems more brilliant
In January.
He waits.
Sitting Crow has brightened the trail
For your failing eyes.
And the Sun has "built fires
Around himself."
To keep you warm
On your travel.

womanhood

love and acceptance

Chapter Six

When I think of love,
I think of love for the land
and love for the gods.
Love is the power that connects
Hawaiians to the land, the sea,
to each other, and to our ancestors.
We are passionate about our culture.
—Lurline Wailana McGregor, Native Hawaiian

The women at this gathering speak of love in grand, sweeping terms that embrace the natural world, family, clan, community, and nation. Love is not limited to immediate family or to a romantic partner. It is not doled out in small increments to a socially prescribed person or group of people. It is all encompassing.

LaDonna Harris speaks eloquently about the high value she places on her relationships with others, which she describes as "not letting go of people," even her adversaries. A Cherokee traditionalist echoes this sentiment and speaks of the need to "live and care for one another in such as a way as to ensure that there will be no reason to let go of others."

The women at this gathering offer the radical notion that sex is more than an exciting surrogate for love. Sex is about whole, healthy relationships, not just technique, bodies, and physical gratification. Dr. Bea Medicine said, "Sexuality is an honorable thing that is just part of life." Given the sheer magnitude of sexual disorders in American society, it would be enormously helpful if more people share the view that making love is "just part of life." A society that values people primarily for their material possessions and physical appearance fosters the idea that transient sexual attraction can be substituted for genuine love and intimacy.

Indigenous women, like their sisters everywhere, are bombarded with the insidious message in magazines, television, and films that only impossibly shaped women are sexually attractive. This has an effect on some women whose sense of self-worth is so tied to their physical appearance that they are unable to enjoy genuine intimacy and love making unless they have perfectly toned bodies. Some women postpone intimate relationships with a partner until they can attain a more ideal appearance as defined by the media. They exercise obsessively, declare war on food, and purchase hundreds of dollars worth of beauty products in pursuit of female perfection. They freeze their faces into expressionless masks with Botox shots and purchase perpetually firm breasts that make them look more like mannequins than humans. And yet it is never enough. Joanne Shenandoah asks, "When will they finally be perfect?" They are bound to fail again and again as they try in vain to look like someone other than themselves. Only a relatively small percentage of the population is naturally thin, yet millions of people in the United States have eating disorders related to self-hatred because of their failure to attain thinness. The popular culture's definition of female beauty as a rail-thin body has precipitated an unprecedented and frightening increase in eating disorders among indigenous youth.

The larger society's endless conversation about whether gay and lesbian couples should be accepted and granted rights to marriage, adoption, and other rights was nonexistent among these women. They place a very high premium on respect: respect for oneself, for others, for all living things. It is highly disrespectful to label another human being and define them based primarily on their sexual preferences. These women care more about the human decency and dignity of people, and whether they are a contributing part of the community, than about their adult relationships with others. Lurline Wailana McGregor speaks about the role of people who transcend gender in Polynesian communities: "In ancient Hawai'i, sexuality was much more free flowing before the imposition of rigid Western moral standards. People were recognized for their individual contributions to the community, not judged by their sexuality. Even today, homosexuality is not the issue in Polynesia that Western society has made of it elsewhere. In American Samoa, I once attended an annual drag queen contest that even government officials participated in judging. Yet there is an increasing stigma about being homosexual because of hypocritical Christian values that abhor such relationships, while at the same time ignoring the hatred and exploitation that such abhorrence generates."

Wilma Mankiller

When I was about six years old, I experienced my first powerful feelings of affection or love, not for a person but for life itself. I don't remember what precipitated the feeling, but I recall sitting in the sun on a rock or log and feeling full of love. Everything seemed perfect in my world. It must have been spring because there were flowers blooming, the air was fresh, and it was a warm, sunny day. Now, more than five decades later, that tremendous affection and love for life still occasionally comes calling. Sometimes I feel it in the stillness of the early morning when I am waiting for the Sun to rise

love and acceptance

over the hills near my home bringing with it the absolute miracle of a new day.

My family taught me a lot about love. My maternal grand-mother was affectionate, loving, irreverent, funny, and would pull me down on her lap even when I was a young adult, although she was about half my size. My parents loved one another and were openly affectionate with one another well after they had grandchil-dren. And both of them, especially my mother, gave all eleven of us children unconditional love. She has been the touchstone and primary champion for all of us, particularly since my father's death in 1971. I now know what a rare gift it was to have parents who did not condition their love on our behavior or personality or even whether they agreed with or entirely understood us. Even when they thought what we were doing was dead wrong or they disagreed with us, they encouraged us to develop our own understanding of things. When my brother Richard decided to leave a lucrative television production training program to join the occupation of Wounded Knee, my mother did not question or judge his decision. She was mostly concerned about his personal safety. I have tried to pass on that same kind of love to my own children, Felicia and Gina, and to my grandchildren. What I learned from my mother is that love is steady, sure, and everlasting. It is not thunder and lightning, a roaring river, or a crashing waterfall. It is a calm, steady stream that never stops flowing. I can't imagine what my life would have been like if I had not always known that there were people who loved me.

When people talk about love, the love of children always comes to mind. It is one of the most wondrous things on Earth. The curiosity, affection, laughter, and hopeful presence of children is an integral part of most meetings and ceremonies I have attended in indigenous com-munities. At Cherokee Ceremonial Grounds and in tradition-oriented societies, the love and respect afforded children is very evident in all aspects of their lives. In 2000, I visited an indigenous women's weaving cooperative in a remote village on the Rio Negro in Brazil. When the women began to gather in a community center to brief us on the cooperative project, the children knew a meeting was at hand and gathered on a large handwoven mat. They stayed on the mat and spoke softly to one another during the entire meeting. When the meeting was over, they scattered and began to play again. I had never seen anything like it. Sarah James said that at the inaugural meeting of the Coalition of Villages that initially met to develop a strategy to defend the Arctic National Wildlife Refuge, the elders wanted the children to be present when they made decisions about the future of the people and the land, so they sent her out to get the children who were swimming. When Sarah told the children they were needed at the meeting, they were more than willing to leave the enjoyment of the swim to attend. They even raced each other to get there.

Love between adults is very complex. Though I have been fortunate to be involved in a relationship where I felt consumed by passion and love, I am not sure I understand the notion of romantic love as defined by American popular culture: diamond rings, roses, champagne, cupid with a harp, and a big wedding. In that context, romantic love seems more like sexual attraction and a contrived fantasy than genuine caring for another person. Sexual attraction is a pretty wonderful thing, but by itself cannot sustain a lifelong commitment. American culture expects people to marry, have children, and confine their love to a tiny nuclear family as if the love would somehow dissipate if it is shared with friends, extended family, the community, the land. Love is a very powerful emotion. Can it be captured and apportioned only to socially acceptable members of the nuclear family?

It is astounding that people sometimes marry one another because they share the same political views or taste in music. That certainly didn't happen to me. My political views are so unique they are shared by almost no one else, and I have never met an indigenous man who likes Gil Scott-Heron or opera. Charlie and I don't listen to music together, and we certainly don't like the same movies. On our first date, he took me to see *Rambo*, which I hate, and to a Coney

love and acceptance

Islander for hot dogs, which I don't like. We are living proof that similar political views and taste in food and music are not the keys to a long-term relationship. We have been together for twenty-two years.

What most people don't understand about our communities is that even with all the hardship and problems, there is an abundance of love among our people. Our traditional leaders, elders, and preachers all instruct us to have love for one another, to view each other as brother and sister. In our communities we depend upon each other for sustenance and support. When one of us is weak, we can lean on others for a time, and the act will be reciprocated by members of the community over and over again during the course of a lifetime. Every winter for the past ten years Charlie has made sure that his brother Johnson has had plenty of firewood for his stove. Charlie deeply appreciated Johnson's help with building a water line in the Bell community. And he is grateful for everything Johnson taught him about what it means to be a Cherokee man. Besides being a loving brother to Johnson, Charlie was a devoted son to his mother, Florence, a spiritually strong and very knowledgeable Cherokee woman who was his greatest teacher and supporter. He lost both Johnson and his mother within days of one another in February of 2004. But he learned a lifetime of lessons about sharing and reciprocity from each of them.

Another example of love and interdependence involves my siblings. When both of my legs were in casts after my automobile accident, my sister Linda cared for me every day for months until I could take care of myself again. Many years later, when she was eligible for disability insurance, I did not hesitate to provide her with assistance. And there is no way I can ever repay my niece Verilee and my brother Louis Donald for donating a kidney to me. I can only try to treasure and honor this precious gift of life they gave me by helping and loving others.

The Gathering
Beatrice Medicine

Love in the larger society is based upon romantic notions and sexuality. Love is a commitment to your family, your larger tiospaye, and the nation as a whole. Sexuality is an honorable thing that is just part of life. We are more concerned with honor than with love. Love is what we feel for each other and the larger unit. But this type of love doesn't have the quality of romantic love, because it is based on a different set of values. So love is honor and living an honorable life that is tied to the values of the group and society. We live by our four cardinal virtues: generosity, fortitude, bravery, and wisdom.

Angela Gonzales

Many people think of love as it relates to their partner or spouse. For me, it is a feeling of warmth I get from my family. That is nonsexual, unconditional love. Often people confuse love with lust. I have had both and I like both, but I see them as very different. At this point, a one-on-one relationship with a partner is not critical to me. That could change.

Sexuality is not something that should be hidden or shameful. It is just a natural part of who we are. Physical attraction is certainly an element of sexuality, but sex is more than sharing one's body for a particular moment. It is a total relationship. Why does it have to only be physical? Why can't it be about the total person? What is disappointing is that Indian men are now starting to think of women in very possessive terms. There is nothing I need to possess.

For a very long time, many women in the larger society around us have felt the need for male acceptance. What worries me is that Indian women now seem to be feeling that as well. And the way they see male acceptance is through physical attraction and personal affirmation in a sexual relationship. To some of the young women I have spoken with, much of

love and acceptance

their sense of self is dependent upon their acceptance by a man. And I have known women who can't be alone. They have to be in a relationship. When one ends, they go in pursuit of another. Or they will be pursuing another relationship when they realize the one they are in is going to end. And to me, that's just really tragic. Why can't women find satisfaction in their own company? What is it about the silence, about being alone, that is so frightening? I love those moments, away from stimulation, noise, and business. Getting into a relationship is more of a choice than a necessity for me.

I have always had this strong sense that I do have agency. I do have control. I am not a victim. I get so frustrated when I hear the "I was born a poor Indian child" speech. I do have choices, and I refuse to be a victim.

Linda Aranaydo

Love is a part of everyone's humanity. A newborn baby has a basic need to be loved and to love back. I would like to be able to express that part of me in everything I do. I have reached a certain age where I don't want to waste time with false hope anymore. It's not helpful to me or to anyone else to do things in a superficial way. So, as a physician, when I am exploring the nature of healing I have to begin with myself. My whole life has been about looking for where the healing lies—for me, and for others.

Love is associated with family in my mind. I haven't had the best of experiences in my two longlasting relationships. My romantic relationships have been stormy and unsatisfying because I wanted to create a family when my partners didn't. When I think of love, I think more of friendship and family, and my grandsons. When my first grandson was born, my heart grew, and that part of me that cares about love and kindness got bigger. A layer of hard feelings fell away, especially toward his grandfather, my former partner.

We had a volatile relationship that lasted six years and produced my two sons. We had lived separate lives for a very long time when our grandson was born. At that point, I didn't even like to be in the same room with him. We went separately to Hawai'i to see the grandbaby. Once I saw him hold our grandson, I let go of a lot of those old negative feelings and accepted his

every day is a good day

place in their lives. Without him, there would be no grandbabies. I'm grateful for my sons and grandsons and new granddaughter on the way. I am grateful that their grandfather loves them and is also a part of their lives. But once I realized he was partially responsible for the fact that Imani exists, I let go of a lot of those negative feelings, and we ended up doing things together.

Love in a romantic relationship would involve people who don't fear each other, who can take risks together, who grow and change and work together to make a family. Maybe I am being very idealistic, because I have not experienced that. I was not always physically safe. I didn't expect the power struggle part. My father and brothers and uncles and cousins were always supportive of me. Unlike many girls, I never had images of growing up and having some big wedding day. I just always thought I would have a family, kids to raise. The physical sexuality, that is easy and natural and just part of life. The difficult part of a relationship for me is the communication, trust, honesty, and accepting each other just the way you are. I have been single for a long time and I'm good at it. It would be nice to have a loving life partner. If it doesn't happen that is okay, because I have lots of love in my life. I think I still fear a broken heart more than any physical "breaking." At least now I know more about living with a broken heart and healing it the best you can.

There is a lot of emphasis now on physical appearance, thinking your physical body is who you are. The house, car, and body are all supposed to reflect a certain image. I went to Mills College, a women's college, for premed, and there were a significant number of women that had anorexia and bulimia. Even the men are now worried about whether they have defined abdominal muscles that they can show off. They don't treat their bodies with kindness or respect but rather like material possessions. I think people need to focus on who they are, and that's not something that can be defined by anything material or physical. I don't really know quite how to define it. Who we are is a kind of awareness, some kind of heart, soul, and spirit that cannot be quantified, that changes and grows every day we interact with the world. Television, magazines, and billboards do not use images of everyday women. Communities need to recognize women in all sizes and shapes so

love and acceptance

young girls can value these women and maybe see the images on television as only passing infatuations with image.

Joanne Shenandoah

Love is an unconditional acceptance of someone, like a mother's love or the love you feel with a partner who will respect you with your flaws. There are no perfect people on this Earth. Children are very easy to love. And sex is a very natural part of life. All women are referred to as Life Givers, which means we have ultimate control over every aspect of the reproductive process from birth control to birthing. Our Native men are at their best when they support these rights.

There are enormous social pressures to be physically beautiful. Some people look at each other on the outside instead of the inside. These people try to have perfect bodies. When are they finally perfect? The most beautiful women I have ever seen are the women in ceremony who dance together. There is nothing more beautiful than the faces of these small, large, young, and old women moving together in a circle. I once read about the Dalai Lama meeting people who were very wealthy and attractive. They had everything they could possibly want yet their existence was so shallow, they required drugs for everything, from waking up to sleeping.

Rosalie Little Thunder

Our Lakota word for love is chantonake, *"to put someone in the heart." It is much bigger than two people in an intimate relationship. Love is wanting good for others and dedication in partnerships. When I think of love, I see one of my grandfathers sitting at grandmother's grave, fifteen years after she went to the Spirit World, smoking a hand-rolled Bull Durham cigarette, watching the pink-gold sunset. He never married again.*

Love is no different in homosexual relationships than in heterosexual ones. The larger society dwells too much on the sexual aspects of homosexual relationships. Can you imagine people being as concerned about the sexual activities of a heterosexual couple? Lakotas don't have any stories about the shaping of our boundaries or values related to homosexuality. A century ago, winktes were considered wakan, or special. They were considered to be gifted and therefore consulted for their insight into the male/female psyche. In a better time, they had a strong role in ceremonial practices too.

Many of my very close friends are winkte males. I am privileged to have a window on the male spirit through the female spirit because of my close friendship with many winkte males. One of these friends offered to teach me the songs that women sing when doing quillwork or beading, which is a rare opportunity in these times. In another experience, I was working on a project and needed an explanation of an issue before giving my consent. I spoke to three men in three separate telephone conversations, and I was getting progressively more confused. I began to suspect something was underfoot. I called the winkte who was part of that project, and he explained it in a straightforward way, ending our conversation with a sigh, "Oh those straight guys!"

Jaune Quick-to-See Smith

Growing up, love was in short supply. I learned about love from my dogs and horses, descriptions in books, my own visceral response to the Sacred, and the occasions when my father was sober and had some to spare. I, like others who have experienced patchy love growing up, tend to look for love in all the wrong places. Having my first child just out of my teens was a big help in developing a sustaining, familial kind of love.

Almost every Indian person I know who is close to my age deals with either their own dysfunction or the dysfunction in the family or both. Rarely do I meet someone my age who claims a living, nurturing family life. Our families have been so ravaged by disease, alcohol, lack of a cohesive culture due to church and government controls, and oppression through discrimination.

My father had such conflict as did most other Indian men who were born around the turn of the century. As a young man he would round up

love and acceptance

wild horses from the white farmers' land, break them, and resell them back to whites. This worked through several marriages with children until the Great Depression hit. At the time I was born, he took labor jobs such as picking hops or herding sheep. I saw my father as a bright, smart, and perceptive man caught up in cultural chaos not of his own making. I loved him no less for his dysfunction. In fact as I grew older, my love became protective toward him. I saw him as fragile, physically and spiritually.

Love entails work and commitment, and love is freely given. Love is a combination of being respectful, forgiving, prayerful, and thankful toward family, friends, tribe, community, and the Sacred.

This brings about my interest in ecosystems and what makes them work. In fact, our families and our tribes are ecosystems—a community together, functioning as a unit. I have been concerned about the disappearing habitat for wild bees and butterflies simply because I've noticed a decline in their population in my yard. I conducted some research and created habitats for black and anise swallowtail butterflies. No matter what the weather or what the season, I head outdoors in the early morning to pray, to watch for the migrations of birds, to be with the Sacred. This too is an expression of love. Thankfulness is the basis of expressing love. A poem by an Eskimo woman, Uvavnuk, comes to mind. It expresses this love better than anything I can conjure up.

> " … *Earth and the great weather*
> *Move me*
> *Have me carried away*
> *And move my inward parts with joy.*"

Lurline Wailana McGregor

In Western society, there is a very narrow concept of love, otherwise there wouldn't be so much hatred and divorce and domestic violence. Sex, which is often confused with love, seems more often engaged in as a means of exerting power, of exploiting others for personal gain than as an expression of love.

every day is a good day

Physical attraction is one thing, but love transcends physical and material attributes. People must embrace the spiritual nature of love if they are to truly know and understand its power. Love can move mountains. It nourishes people's souls more profoundly than material acquisitions could ever hope to do. We as Hawaiians are very fortunate to live in such a powerful environment and to be able to still call upon our rich spiritual heritage to help us, even today.

Gail Small

Cheyenne people are very oriented toward imagery. Imagery, not words, is everything to us. We are taught to use imagery when we hear the stories. So when I think of love, the image that immediately develops is one of my parents, my children, and the rest of my family. My first love was my parents, and I am so fortunate that they are well and continue to love us. It gives us strength. Also, when I think of love, I think about the land. Cheyenne homeland is so strong, it strengthens us. When I am weak or tired, I just want to go home. Families have certain areas that are very special to them, where the spirits reside. They will take care of us and we will take care of them.

Octaviana Valenzuela Trujillo

Love means responsibility—responsibility to keep loved ones happy and without disappointment. Love does not come easy, as it has too many responsibilities.

Faith Smith

Love is how I feel about the people I would give whatever I have— time or money. There are no boundaries of my emotional, material, and spiritual investment. I don't just mean my son and granddaughter, mother, aunts, and uncles. There are other people who are not closely related, but they

love and acceptance

are part of my family. I cannot imagine life without them. These are the
people who understand me, know my warts, love me, care for me, and are
willing to nurture me and share whatever they have.

Joy Harjo

Love is about acceptance and compassion. It's about being able to
see through the various levels of this Earth experience—through the violence,
the striving, jealousy, anger, to the truth of it. I have experienced it through
my babies and with people I am close to, and transcendentally, even through
relative strangers. Once on a packed subway in New York City my heart
became the beefy Germanic construction worker who sat squished in, with
his paint- and grease-spattered lunchbox between his feet. I don't know how
to explain it. I became him, without judgment. He was someone I normally
would not strongly relate to. The overall sense was rooted in compassion,
or vnokeckv.

Love is the most powerful force in the world. It cannot be destroyed.
Love is where we come from and where we are going. When people plant
food, they learn to love the plants as they come up, and they learn to love
the Earth and connect with it. That connection was broken for everyone when
they all started buying food at the store.

I grew up thinking love and sex were the same. My mother and her
friends were fixed on schemes about attracting and keeping a man. I always
remember my mother exclaiming, "If I ever get married again, it will be to a
woman." She denies it now. That comment came because they were closer to
each other than they were to the cocksure men in their lives. In my younger
life, I got into some really tough times because I thought sex was love, and
I just wanted attention. I was never taught how to channel my sensuality.
It took me a long time to learn that sexuality was about connection and a
higher love. The connection between two people is part of an amazing process
of creating a new generation of ideas, art, or children.

We all have parts of our lives that are disaster areas, or what I call

every day is a good day

blind spots. In my case, the area marked "love and sexuality" is a soap opera of epic proportions. I do have a wild streak, which I inherited from my father. Is it a wild streak or a genetic flaw? Or a gene designed for invention, for comic relief, or tragic endings?

Last night I dreamed that a group of Native women activists were all in a bus riding together. I was sitting at the back of the bus and I could see everyone. Toward the front, I could see this old Native woman, probably Hawaiian, and she was talking, but I soon realized nobody else could see her. She was a little angry, but compassionate, saying, "You know it is important that you remember to pray. You have to remember who you are. You need to go out and plant. You need to remember this is how you connect. This is how you will know you who are. You have to plant to be part of this. You have to remember these teachings whether you are Cherokee, Muscogee Creek, or Native Hawaiian." It's all about respect. It is about love, about understanding the continuum, and understanding how to respect one another. There is a certain decorum, or aloha, on how you treat other human beings.

Mary and Carrie Dann

Love is what we feel for the children. I think about respect, trust, honor, and the things that make people want to get along with each other. That is my definition of love. People say, "I love you." What does that mean? It is hollow. White people do not understand love. When I think about love, I think about respect, trust, honor, whatever makes people want to get along with each other. When you wrap this up, then you have love. That's my definition of love.

From what I understand from the Western Shoshone people, the women were once thought of in a different light than today. One would rarely hear about a male violating the women. That violation only came during the time of the white settlers.

love and acceptance

Audrey Shenandoah

Being good to everybody is love. My grandma taught me never to dislike anybody. She said even if someone does not like you, it doesn't cost you anything to greet them. It must be terrible to hate something or hate somebody. It must be an awful feeling. I can understand it when people say hate will consume you, because it makes people unhappy when they don't like someone.

Our people have been influenced by the world around us. The word sex *has only come into use in the past twenty years. Making love was never called sex before that. Now the word* sex *is just thrown around, and people have no respect for love. My goodness, people change partners almost with the wind. One night with one person, and the next night with another. And that's really sad. But since the word* sex *has been substituted, it has made a difference. My twelve-year-old grandson asked me, "What is sex?" I told him sex is how you describe the gender of a person.*

Sarah James

In Gwich'in we say che gwin von. *That means "love for everything." There is no limit for love and we can't love anything more than the Creator. Everything he makes is good. Therefore, we have love for everything. Love is not just directed toward an individual but also includes the Creator and everything in the world.*

Ella Mulford

Love means peace. I see a waterfall, I hear birds singing, water swishing off the rocks, a wind breezing through the leaves, and there are smiles on the faces of people. We have a choice between love and fear. Love comes with positive results, and fear is associated with negative emotions such as hate, anger, and jealousy. It seems like a simple choice to make, but obviously some people don't see it that way since we are experiencing so many wars on our planet.

LaDonna Harris

My grandmother who raised me showed love and affection, she honored her relationships with people, and she was admired and respected because of the way she treated people. When my grandmother and I walked down the street in Walters, Oklahoma, people greeted her in a very reverential way. And none of the people who smoked cigarettes would smoke or take a drink in front of her, because they knew she didn't approve of it. She commanded that kind of respect. When I was with her, I felt a great sense of belonging, because so many people seemed to be related to us by blood or by a lengthy relationship. Being with her gave me the sense that if I treated people right and behaved myself, people would also respect me. When I come home to reconnect to my extended family and friends, I am deeply touched when people say, "you remind me of your grandmother."

My grandmother also taught me a lot about honoring relationships. Fred and I had a wonderful, supportive network of friends and family, and many of those relationships have been maintained. Even though we are now divorced, Fred and I are the best of friends. We spend Thanksgiving and Christmas together, and his wife cooks supper for all of us. We make her feel comfortable. It is important to me and to my children to keep that relationship with Fred. I never think about losing anybody, even an adversary. I may never have them as a close friend, but I don't lose them. People in my life are valuable. In the Comanche way, if you have hurt someone, you will also be hurt until you go back and try to reinstate that relationship or make it right in some way.

love and acceptance

Florence Soap

I consider myself a prayerful person. When I pray, I always pray to love all people. Some people claim that they love, but it is not from their heart. By carefully observing a person, one can tell if they have love within them. I pray that people will learn to love one another.

the way home

Chapter Seven

A nation is not conquered until the hearts
of its women are on the ground.
Then it is done, no matter how brave
its warriors or strong its weapons.
—Cheyenne proverb

In the face of almost overwhelming economic and social problems, most of the women at this gathering remain hopeful about the future. While each has chosen a unique path for her life and work, all have waged a lifelong battle to restore health and wholeness to their communities. Several women spoke about their personal resolve to lead a meaningful, purposeful life and to be a good person.

It is remarkable that indigenous women continue to value traditional knowledge and original institutions after their people have endured war, removal, loss of land, resources, and rights, and wholesale attempts at assimilation. If they continue to have strong, viable communities and manage to hold onto a robust sense of who they are despite the staggering amount of adversity they have faced, they can surely be confident that 500 years from now there will be culturally distinct communities of indigenous people on these lands.

After every major tribalwide upheaval, they have almost had to reinvent themselves as a people—but they have never given up their sense of community, of clan, of family, of nation. The story of the renaissance of Cherokee people after the infamous Trail of Tears is similar in some ways to the story of tenacious indigenous people everywhere. It illustrates the ability of a battered people to not just survive but despite everything, to thrive. It could be the story of any indigenous community.

There were many precipitating factors for the Cherokee removal, including racism and greed. However, states rights' advocates, including leaders of the infant state of Georgia, were the strongest proponents of Cherokee removal. Leading up to the removal, Georgia leaders provided for a survey of Cherokee land and a lottery to distribute that land to white Georgians.

Angry Georgians found a vigorous champion of states' rights and Cherokee removal in President Andrew Jackson, who took office in 1829. Jackson soon urged the passage of legislation to enable removal of the Cherokee Nation and other southeastern tribes. After bitter debate, Jackson's Indian Removal Act of 1836 passed, authorizing the president to establish districts west of the Mississippi in exchange for Indian-held land in the Southeast.

Cherokee people overwhelmingly opposed the Removal Act, refusing to leave their homelands voluntarily. With no authorization from the Cherokee people, a small band of proremoval Cherokees signed the Treaty of New Echota, agreeing to the land exchange. In 1838, the U.S. Army began the process of forcing Cherokee people from their homelands to Indian Territory. By the time the removal ended in April of 1839, approximately 4,000 Cherokee people—almost one-fourth of the entire Cherokee population—had died either while being held in stockades or during the removal process, which was conducted in all seasons, including the cold winter months and the extreme heat of the summer. Because of the devastating toll in lives and land, the Cherokee removal is often referred to as the Trail of Tears or the Trail Where They Cried.

What gives me hope and strength is to remember how our people—reeling from terrible losses and separated from everything familiar to them—created life anew after the Trail of Tears. Cherokees in Indian Territory soon began rebuilding their families, their communities, and the Cherokee Nation. They developed a sophisticated judicial system, created an extensive educational system with schools for both boys and girls, printed newspapers in Cherokee and English, and erected beautiful institutions of government that stand today as some of the oldest buildings in what is now Oklahoma. In the early twentieth century, there were a number of unsuccessful legislative attempts to abolish the Cherokee Nation, which one hundred years later is a thriving tribal government.

After several hundreds of years of sustained opposition to the continuation of our government and our unique lifeways, we rejoice in the knowledge that ceremonies given to us by the Creator continue, the original languages are still spoken, and our governments remain strong. Octaviana Valenzuela Trujillo says, "Our resiliency in the face of overwhelming historical, political, cultural, and social challenges in our adopted U.S. homeland is a tremendous feat. We have been tenacious in surviving as a distinct people."

We acknowledge the hardships of the past without dwelling on them every day. Instead, we look to the future with the same faith that kept us together thus far. To be sure, some indigenous languages have vanished while others are endangered. Some of the old ceremonies have been lost over time, and our communities are no longer as intact as they once were—but in most tribal communities, even the most troubled and acculturated, there are indigenous people who continue to use ancient knowledge to inform their lives. Their relationship to and interdependence with every other living thing—humans, animals, the stars, the land—is held together by a common understanding of history, culture, and most importantly, values. Traditional stories passed from generation to generation as well as ceremonies and rituals contribute to indigenous people's understanding of their place in the universe. Audrey Shenandoah described the ceremonies that reinforce thankfulness, respectfulness, and peace of mind as "holding the people" until the next ceremony. Because indigenous people still connect with a distinct community, they have a strong sense of identity, belonging, and understanding their place in the universe. Joy Harjo says, "I have a home in the world. I feel there is a root community that I have a responsibility to nurture and help move in a good direction. It's very, very precious. It is the central source of meaning, the root, the template."

Tribal elders have expressed concern that the traditional values and ceremonies that have sustained us since the beginning of time are now "slipping away." Many tribal communities have made it a priority to recapture, protect, and maintain traditional tribal knowledge systems and lifeways that are often described as a whole or interconnected way of viewing things. The environment is not seen as a social justice issue but as an essential element of all life. Rosalie Little Thunder says, "We are in a time when human beings have forgotten our place. Many humans behave as though we are masters of all there is, that everything exists just for our comfort and convenience." Not just indigenous people but all human beings evolved from people who understood their reciprocal relationship to their extended families and to all other living things. Over time, others have adopted the nuclear family model. Many have lived in an artificial world completely separate from the natural world for so long, they have little understanding of their place in the world and do not seem to understand that everything in the natural world is integral to the continuation of human life on Earth. How many people living in high-rises and rushing about in cities even notice that the Sun rises in the east and sets in the west? How can they dream if their bare feet never touch the earth and they never behold the miracle of the stars?

When the women at this gathering talk about revitalizing their communities, they talk about starting small businesses, protecting the natural world, getting better access to good health care, technology, and a solid education. But they also talk about restoring balance and harmony in their families and communities. Some communities have initiated aggressive projects to preserve tribal culture and heritage. The Blackfeet, with the able leadership of Darrell Kipp, started a highly successful language immersion school; the Onondaga School teaches tribal history and language; the Hopi Foundation works to protect ancient tribal knowledge and structures; and the Cherokee language is taught in many communities, in language immersion programs, and through Cherokee Nation Head Start programs.

More and more, we trust our own thinking instead of deferring to Bureau of Indian Affairs officials or well-meaning outsiders, and we are looking within our own communities for solutions to entrenched problems. In response to the shocking number of indigenous people who do not complete a course of higher education, tribal people have developed an extensive system of tribal community colleges. Tribally controlled community colleges have made a profound difference in the overall educational level of tribal people. Tribal communities and governments are issuing their own passports; running their own enterprises, health clinics, and hospitals; certifying their own foster homes; handling their own adoptions; negotiating their own leases; and taking charge of their future. The American Indian Science and Engineering Society has produced Native scientists, physicians, and practitioners of the hard sciences while reinforcing the value of traditional knowledge.

The Institute of American Indian Arts in Santa Fe has spawned several generations of award-winning artists who are reshaping the image of Native Americans and destroying the age-old stereotypes of indigenous people as either mystical children of nature incapable of higher thought or bloodthirsty pagans. The Institute is now undertaking building of a lifelong learning center to serve as a sort of indigenous think tank. Indigenous authors, journalists, filmmakers, museum curators, historians, professors, and secondary-school educators are changing public perceptions of indigenous people. They all accept their responsibility to make sure the unborn will always know what it means to be descendants of the original people of this land.

Wilma Mankiller

The question I am asked most frequently is why I remain such a positive person, after surviving breast cancer, lymphoma, dialysis, two kidney transplants, and systemic myasthenia gravis. The answer is simple: I am Cherokee, and I am a woman. No one knows better than I that every day is indeed a good day. How can I be anything but positive when I come from a tenacious, resilient people who keep moving forward with an eye toward the future even after enduring unspeakable hardship? How can I not be positive when I have lived longer than I ever dreamed possible and my life plays itself out in a supportive community of extended family and friends? There is much to be thankful for. Though I am an ordinary woman, I have been blessed with many extraordinary experiences. I have been privileged to travel extensively, meet world leaders like Nelson Mandela, represent tribal people in meetings with several United States presidents, and work with visionary tribal leaders and activists.

I learned at a fairly early age that I cannot always control the things that are sent my way or the things that other people do, but I can most certainly control how I think about them and react to them. I don't spend a lot of time dwelling on the negative. I believe that having a good, peaceful mind is the basic premise for a good life. My sense of faith, hope, and optimism stems in part from being a Cherokee woman and in part from a cool November morning in 1978.

After a quick glance at the morning news, I poured a cup of coffee and headed out the door. I had no idea my life would soon change forever. About three miles from my home, I started up a slight grade. On the other side of the hill, my friend Sherrye Morris pulled out to pass two slow-moving cars. When I came to the top of the hill, her car was in my lane. Our cars hit head on. I have very little

every day is a good day

recollection of what happened immediately after the accident. I was in shock from my injuries and loss of blood. I vaguely remember there was blood everywhere, and people were screaming. By the time an ambulance took the driver of the other car, Sherrye, to Tahlequah, her life had already slipped away. I was taken by ambulance to Stilwell, where I was stabilized and then transferred to a regional hospital in Fort Smith, Arkansas. As the ambulance sped toward Fort Smith, death beckoned me with an intense overall feeling of peacefulness and warmth. I felt a carefree lightness and an overpowering pull toward an unconditional, all-encompassing love. Everything in that world was perfect. I had begun a beautiful and sacred journey toward the land of the Creator when my daughters, Felicia and Gina, came into my mind, and I returned to this world. That near-death experience made a significant difference in the way I have lived my life. After that, I no longer feared death, and I no longer feared life.

Now from a distance of more than two decades, I look back on that terrible November day and wonder what Sherrye's life would have been like if she could have lived beyond her early thirties and been able to watch her sensitive, smart daughter, Meghan, grow into a focused young woman who works on a range of social justice issues. And I wonder what my life would have been like if the Creator had not sent so many challenges my way.

The first challenge after the accident was learning that one leg was so badly crushed that amputation was a possibility, and permanent disability was very probable. The other leg was broken in several places, and my face and chest were crushed. Though no one spoke about it, I knew there had been another car involved in the accident. After three weeks in the hospital, I was coming to grips with my injuries when Mike Morris gave me the devastating news about his wife, Sherrye. There are no words to describe the disbelief and pain I experienced during the next days, weeks, and months as I dealt with Sherrye's death and my own extensive injuries. By the time I had recovered enough to return to work, I had endured seventeen separate surgeries, mostly on my legs. I was once told that the most lovely and precious flowers can be seen only in the bottom of a very deep valley. I have been in that valley and seen those incredible flowers. The steep climb out of the valley made me stronger and more mature. After that it was hard to envision what it would take to really rattle me. I am convinced that those experiences prepared me for the position of principal chief of the Cherokee Nation and for the other challenges that awaited me.

When I returned to work eighteen months after the accident, our principal chief, Ross Swimmer, assigned me the task of working with a team to develop self-help housing and water projects in rural historic Cherokee communities. Working primarily with Charlie Soap, a bilingual Cherokee with a reputation for being able to "get things done," we developed several successful projects in a number of communities. All of that work validated my belief that Cherokee people are mutually supportive and willing to help each other. After these projects were completed, it would be difficult for anyone to ever again argue that Cherokees did not have the capacity to solve their own problems, given the resources and right set of circumstances. Based on our work in communities, the Cherokee Nation Community Development Department was formed, and I became its founding director, a position I held until 1983 when Ross Swimmer bypassed all his male political allies and chose me for his running mate.

Ross Swimmer and I were quite the team. He is a Republican. I am a Democrat. In those days, Cherokee candidates put together a slate or team of candidates for all elective offices: principal chief, deputy principal chief, and fifteen legislators or members of the tribal council. By the time I informed Ross Swimmer I would accept his offer to seek the office of deputy principal chief, all his council slate had been chosen, and they all opposed my candidacy—but none more than the Swimmer team campaign manager, Councilman Gary Chapman. Chapman had hoped to be chosen to run as deputy chief on Ross Swimmer's ticket, but Swimmer disqualified him because both he and Chapman were senior officials of the First National Bank, a depository of Cherokee Nation funds. The Swimmer/Mankiller campaign was run out of Chapman's garage.

So I faced opposition from within the Swimmer campaign as well as from the two other candidates who filed for the office of deputy principal chief. On more than one occasion, Charlie Soap, my future husband, tried to convince me that Swimmer's people were not campaigning for me or even supporting me. Though I knew they did not support me, I refused to accept the notion that some of Swimmer's people were actively working against me. Once, Ross Swimmer called to ask me if I had been campaigning in bars, something I would not even remotely consider. The source of this rumor was Gary Chapman. Toward the end of the campaign, I was asked by Swimmer's campaign workers to take campaign-related information to the Stilwell newspaper. Out of curiosity, I opened the manila envelope and discovered ads for Ross Swimmer for chief and my opponent, J. B. Dreadfulwater, for deputy principal chief. Charlie was right. I finally got it!

Charlie and I developed our own campaign strategy, and we both worked very hard right up until two weeks before the election when Charlie had to leave for an overseas trip. A small crew of volunteers, along with my mother, my girls, and my brothers and sisters, worked until we were exhausted. My brother Jim had an old van that we loaded up with signs to put up along country roads. On the day of the election, I decided not to stay at the "watch party" with the Swimmer campaign group. Instead, I went to Tallahassee Muscogee Creek Ceremonial Grounds and danced until the Sun came up. In the morning, I called Tahlequah and learned that Ross Swimmer had won the election and that I faced Agnes Cowen in a run-off election. After a relatively uneventful campaign, I won the run-off election.

When Ross Swimmer resigned in 1985 to take a position in Washington, D.C., I moved into the position of principal chief to fill out his term. It was up to the tribal council to fill the vacant position of deputy chief from their ranks. The names of three candidates emerged: Clarence Sunday, a respected elder and former associate of Chief Bill Keeler; John Ketcher, a sixty-two-year-old bilingual Cherokee; and Gary Chapman. Two weeks before the council meeting in which my successor would be chosen, I asked my old nemesis, Chapman, if he was a candidate for deputy chief, and he denied any interest in the position. Then just before the council meeting, a friend called me in Washington, D.C., to inform me of a plan by some members of the council to seat Chapman, and then remove me from office. Chapman would then become principal chief, and one of his supporting council members would become deputy chief. I thought this was just another political rumor but decided to check it out anyway. I quickly discovered Chapman was indeed a candidate for deputy chief and had the commitment of most council members. At that time I did not know whether Chapman was leading an effort to oust me so he could become principal chief or if he just wanted to become deputy chief. Whatever his motives, I knew that if he obtained the position, he would oppose me at every opportunity. I flew home from Washington the night before the council meeting, and Charlie and I went to work on the telephone, slept for a couple of hours, and got on the telephone again first thing in the morning. Our goal was to stop Chapman and find a viable alternative candidate. First I called John Ketcher and asked him to remain a candidate. I asked John to work on the three undecided council members while I called the others. Meanwhile, Sunday agreed to support Ketcher. The next morning, I sat in the council chambers and watched the council members file in with full knowledge that my political future in the Cherokee Nation was at stake. Chapman and his supporters appeared confident, jostling and joking with one another.

The successful deputy chief candidate had to receive two-thirds of the vote of the council. From the outset the vote was split between Ketcher and Chapman. The council recessed, negotiated, and voted again. The vote was the same. A member of the council asked who would work best with me. People around me advised me to remain neutral because I had to work with whomever the council selected.

Not being very familiar with neutrality, I stood up and gave John Ketcher my unequivocal support. The council recessed again, negotiated, and voted again. The vote had not changed, and it was clear that no change was in sight. At that time Chapman withdrew his candidacy. The council then immediately voted unanimously for Ketcher, one of the finest men I know.

John and I served out the rest of that term, and we were elected for two more four-year terms. In 1994 both John Ketcher and I decided against seeking office in the upcoming 1995 elections. After working many years as an employee of the nation and then serving three four-year terms in elective office, I decided it was time for a change for me and for the Cherokee Nation. And, I had a nagging feeling that something was physically wrong.

Six months after I left office, while serving as a Montgomery Fellow at Dartmouth College, I was diagnosed with second-stage lymphoma. Since there were no comparable treatment facilities near my home in Oklahoma, I remained in Boston for almost eight months while undergoing chemotherapy treatments. My world suddenly shifted and narrowed considerably. A year earlier Diné (Navajo) Chairman Peterson Zah and I had led a delegation to meet with President Clinton on behalf of all tribal nations. Now my days were spent poring over the results of bone scans, gallium scans, X-rays, waiting to learn whether my white and red blood cell counts were up or down and seeing whether the chemotherapy had shrunk the tumor. During the time I was being treated for lymphoma, I was being sued by the very controversial Joe Byrd administration, which succeeded me at the Cherokee Nation in 1995. Joe Byrd and the tribal council eventually dropped the civil suit against me for granting severance pay to employees who left when my term of office ended, citing incorrect information as the reason they had initiated the lawsuit. But by then I had already spent thousands of dollars to defend myself and months alternating between chemotherapy treatments and responding to dozens of interrogatories and motions. Once I had to fly back to

Oklahoma for a deposition where I faced a battery of lawyers for Byrd, including Susan Plumb, Gary Chapman's daughter.

That time in Boston was very difficult. For the first time in my life, I felt completely alone and vulnerable as I defended myself against my own body and external threats such as the lawsuit. Though many people loved and rallied around me, that period of illness and feeling attacked from every possible front was a solitary journey. Even the most empathetic healthy person cannot fully understand the tremendous emotional, intellectual, and physical changes that occur when you are diagnosed with a serious illness. During this time of trauma and stress, I was 2,000 miles away from my family and community in a place where nothing was familiar. It was extremely disorienting. I learned a lot from the experience, mostly about myself. I never lost my sense of determination or humor during that period. I still laugh when I remember being suddenly frightened and startled when I unexpectedly caught a glimpse of my bald, pale, thin self in a mirror.

I willed myself to remain spiritually strong through prayer, meditation, and relaxation exercises. I sang, played guitar, and tried to do something positive every day. After chemotherapy, radiation, and stem cell transplants, the lymphoma became quiet. Once I was able to return to my home in Mankiller Flats, surrounded by the land that I love, the first thing I did was walk to the freshwater spring of my childhood, sit in my usual spot facing east, and say a heartfelt prayer of thanksgiving that I was able to come full circle to this special place where my life began.

The Gathering
Sarah James

We have to make real changes in our own lives and in our communities. In order to protect our tribes, we must respect our health and the
environment. We are the caretakers of the Earth. Let's act as such and make
the changes we need to improve our land and teach others to do the same. We
have to walk our talk. We have to go back to living a clean life and having
clear air, clean water, and a functioning ecosystem. We have to learn to reuse,
recycle, use less energy, and share more. I believe a healthy environment is
a basic human right. Our right to survive is a basic, sacred, fundamental
human right.

We should be proud that we made it this far as a people, and we
should teach that to our people so they understand who we were before
and who we are today. We should also teach others about our people and
our ways.

We should assure that a true account of our history is taught in
all Native and non-Native schools. We must teach our children to be proud
of who they are and where they come from. They come from a people who
believe it is important to respect oneself and respect the Earth. They come
from a people who work hard, who pray, who fight for the land, who have
our own language, who are good people with strong families. We must teach
them to speak in our Native languages. We should make sure our children
know they will never be homeless. They have a home in this world and a
responsibility that was given to them by the Creator. They are important to
their people. We also must educate non-Native children about who we are
and foster respect for each other, and we must help find the common ground
between all people.

We must work to change institutions that create power imbalances.
We must gain a voice in all decisions that affect our lives. Those who control
health care and education control us. Our indigenous nations have a right
to take over all federal service contracts in order to have a voice in education,

the way home

health care, our justice systems, and social services while we strengthen our economies. This is the right thing to do.

Audrey Shenandoah

It is the spiritual beliefs that have always enabled us to persevere, and those beliefs have kept our people together. There has always been a nucleus of people who are strong in our tradition, our customs, and with the language and the ceremonies.

But overall, we have lost our sense of balance. Keeping balance between the real things in life and a respectful mind is very important. If people get an education, a good position, and money, they need to do the right things and help the people, not only our own people, but all of humanity. Maintaining our spiritual values is very important. A lack of spiritual values causes people a lot of problems. People are so busy working and making money, they don't have time to spend on spiritual matters.

There are many crucial issues here—the land claims, the water, health care. For many years, our waters have been abused and used as a cesspool. I am also concerned about the way our people are deteriorating as Haudenosaunee, Original People. They are following ways that can only lead to destruction. Some of our people are making lots of money, not caring for their family or others, and abusing themselves with drugs and alcohol. Every family is affected by this problem.

Mary and Carrie Dann

We need to ensure that our spiritual life and cultural life are cared for and protected. If we lose our spiritual ways, forget about all the other little spiritual beings out there, we have done ourselves in. There is no other religion or form of worship besides that of Native Americans that includes every living thing.

People need to get out of their warm house and see what the Earth is all about. They need to see what is happening to the Earth and all the destruction caused by humans. They need to see where the water comes from and what is happening to the water. Maybe with a lot of teaching the balance can be restored. Some of the things scientists do are wacky. They have no common sense. A lot of the things they do lead to destruction of humans and our other relations that live outside. People have got to get up and go see that for themselves. If people are lonesome, it is their own fault. They have all of Earth's children around them. Maybe you can't have a conversation with them, but they are there and can translate whatever you are saying and thinking. They are part of you, and you are part of them.

In the summertime people go from air-conditioned houses to air-conditioned cars to an air-conditioned office or workplace. In the winter, they go from a warm house to a warm car to a warm office, and everything is too comfy. They have no idea of what other little life is out there. They don't know that in order to wear a gold ring, somebody's spiritual home might have been destroyed to get to the gold. When mining for Black Hills gold, they are destroying a place that is important to the spiritual beliefs of the Lakota people. People no longer think about these things. They get bottled water from the shelves of grocery stores because we have polluted our water. If you think about these things, you have to wonder, in what direction is the human race going?

Some people are intellectually smart, but they have lost their identity. They don't know where they are coming from or where they are going.

I want our great-grandchildren to know the Western Shoshone ways and to speak our language. I want them to be thankful for their lives. I don't want them to worship money or to be a part of the lost generation that no longer knows who they are.

Florence Soap

It is important that we keep knowledge about Cherokee medicine, the real medicine. When the older people die, they take the medicine with them. Young people today don't want to learn about our culture. They like to learn the ways of the white people. God gave the white people a language, *the Creeks a language, and the Cherokee a language. We should speak our own language.*

Family and kinship relationships are important. I am of the Wolf Clan, and if I go to North Carolina and I tell them I am of the Wolf Clan, they get excited because they have found a relative.

Joy Harjo

In order to live I had to make peace with being Muscogee Creek in this world. I had to make peace with being female in this world. I had to make peace with being a light-skinned Indian in this world. I've had to make peace with my flaws and tendencies. I continue working on how to transform destruction into something beautiful and useful. The overriding theme of my life has been transformation and how to keep moving, despite the tests. I am concerned with how to grow imagination and actively participate in the regeneration of cultures through art. I have failed more than I have succeeded, and have learned that failure is the fertilizer.

Each community has a particular shape, spirit, and integrity, whether it's the Tallahassee Ceremonial Grounds, which I belong to, or Okmulgee or Tiger Flats. That community is where I have my roots even though I go to California, Hawai'i, or other places. My medicine maker at Tallahassee Grounds described me as an ambassador, and I feel that in the work I do. My work is not just about me.

There is something very powerful that created the struggle that got Creek and Cherokee people to Indian Territory from our homelands in the Southeast. That power also created that little community of Tallahassee outside of Okmulgee. We were tested terribly. To make myself feel better about everything that has happened to our people, I have to think that we were very much loved, or we wouldn't have survived.

The biggest challenge for the future is for all of us to try to be better human beings. Being a good human being is an art. While I am working on my music, poetry, or stories, I am constantly diving down and coming back with amazing things that are much larger than I am. I started writing things

every day is a good day

down and sometimes I am literally hanging on to my pen. Even as a young child I liked the idea of making a mark and making something appear, sort of like magic. The consistent theme in my art is compassion. It is harder to have compassion for myself than it is to have compassion for other people. At times I am very hard on myself. I used to have a lot of self-hatred, which goes back to my father's inability to love himself. I also realize the utter destruction that occurred in this country. My work is not just about me. If the people have stories about me someday, I hope they will say Joy Harjo was a good human being who loved people.

Linda Aranaydo

Three days before my fiftieth birthday, I went back to the old Creek Nation in Alabama and Georgia, the original homelands of my people before their forced removal to Oklahoma. I wanted to go to those places and see what the land was like, how the land was doing. And I thought there was some healing there for me. I brought an abalone shell filled with medicine from California to the mound, and I prayed. I said prayers for my family and asked my ancestors to help us be well, and I let them know that we continued. I let them know we hadn't abandoned them, and that we remembered them and their love. I prayed to let go of anger and resentment. Before that, I could never read Creek history because it made me so angry. Grandpa's stories made me cry. I asked myself if anger is the legacy I want to leave my grandchildren. I want them to know all the different cultures that have come together to make them, my rainbow babies, my four directions babies, but I want them to know how to be a human without bitterness or anger. Negative emotions are like handcuffs that keep us from creating or trying something new.

It is important for the medical community to develop ways to treat people with kindness and respect, to take care of a total human being by paying attention to their emotions and their state of mind as well as their physical components. Right now there are few models of truly integrated systems. Each individual medical practitioner needs to give up illusions about

the way home

having power over how other people behave. The sort of universe anyone has control over is internal. It is up to each of us individually to work to find balance. They will find their balance in families and communities, in relationship with the full natural world. I can provide some advice or make my home and my clinic a place that nurtures balance. People need quiet time away from the busy images and the noise of the materialistic world.

Gail Small

Supporting our children and families will help restore the balance. To the Cheyenne, family life is important. To me, a two-parent family is critical. Children that have not had a two-parent family have a harder time. When I was growing up at Northern Cheyenne, the families of my parents—aunts, uncles, grandparents, and other extended family members—were involved with me on a daily basis. They would provide for me and discipline me. I would not be where I am today without their help. The best thing I can give my teenage daughters is a sense of who they are and where they come from. The world is moving very fast and they are in so many worlds, it is important that they know they have a home, a place where they can be safe and can renew their strength. They are young, and will experiment with different cultures as they move in and out of these different worlds, but they will get through it because they are very secure in who they are. The oldest daughter in the Cheyenne family has a huge role in perpetuating the culture and maintaining the family, so it is important that she is grounded in her understanding of her homeland and has a strong sense of who she is and where she is from.

To make sure there is a good world for the future, we have to work on many fronts. We are very concerned about the severe environmental damage that will be done by coal-bed methane gas, a form of natural gas that is in demand as a clean-burning fuel. The methane is found in coal seams held in place by water pressure. Extracting the methane requires removal of groundwater to reduce pressure in the coal beds. There are more than 325 new methane gas well permits pending approval on the Northern Cheyenne and Crow Reservations, both of which have large deposits of underground aquifers that supply water. Methane gas threatens the very existence of our homelands.

Language and culture are also important. With each loss of an elder, we become more concerned about protecting the Cheyenne language. Only about 30 to 40 percent of our people still speak the Cheyenne language, about half of whom are over 40 years of age. Cheyenne people, who are raised in intergenerational families with a grandparent living in the home, are more likely to speak the language. Everyone has a responsibility to make the Cheyenne language a priority—the tribal government, the family, the schools, and the community. We worked for three decades to get a high school on the reservation. Now the high school plans to work in collaboration with Dull Knife Memorial College to support and maintain Cheyenne language by developing curriculum and establishing language courses.

Faith Smith

These days, it is not just outsiders but some of the people in our own communities who are making decisions that run counter to the values of respect. They say a lot of good words about taking care of the elders, respecting them and their wisdom, and yet their actions don't reflect that respect. In our community, the elders have become a very active political force. They are putting pressure on tribal governments to think about their actions in relation to elders. The casinos are an issue. How can these resources be used in a way that really builds the fabric of the community and not individual wealth and class? The creation of a class system has been happening in indigenous communities for a long time, but the pace has been accelerated because the dollars involved are so much greater now.

We have to do more work to eliminate racism and negative stereotypes about Indian people. I used to think the most important thing we could do is educate the general public about Indian people. This was based on the premise that if they knew us better, they would act in a positive, responsible way to address issues that impact us. Now, I think it is much deeper than that. It requires a broader agenda and work at multiple levels. It is difficult work. People can have a lot of factual information about Indians and remain indifferent to these facts and hold on to their foolish notion that to be Indian is to be a drunk on the street.

The values that measure whether a society is great are very different in our communities. We value our kinship relations, a sense of who we are, and a connection to our community. Their measures are economic: what kind of car or home they have and how much they paid for it.

The hostility toward Indian people is greater in towns and businesses that border Indian reservations. They depend on tribal people for their very economy, but some are openly hostile to Indian people. In the city, it is much more subtle because there are other people of color here. But there are stereotypes about them as well.

Once a Japanese researcher visited our college for several summers, interviewing a lot of tribal people so he could gain firsthand knowledge of the Native American experience. He also went to the Chicago Board of Education to ask them why they were not providing the support necessary to keep Native American children from dropping out. Some of the people actually said, "They're too dumb." We had been working with the Chicago Board of Education for thirty years, and still they make the broad judgment that our tremendously bright kids are too dumb.

I do what I can to restore balance in our communities. I want to be remembered as a woman of the people, of the community, and as someone who had a good purpose in life.

Octaviana Valenzuela Trujillo

Balance in our communities can be recovered through a reintegration of our traditional ways. Our indigenous languages express the spiritual balance inherent in our traditional lifeways. Their utilization therefore leads to restoring that balance by reconnecting us to our indigenous roots through giving expression to concepts and notions that are not readily translatable. Traditional ways of expressing our relationship to other humans and nonhuman entities in the natural kingdom help to keep us in balance, and in fact, constitute the underpinnings of the spirituality of indigenous peoples.

The loss of identity is the greatest challenge faced by indigenous people in the twenty-first century. Identity encompasses our culture and sense of place—where and how we connect to the physical and spiritual world. It is conceptualized and articulated through our language. Many indigenous peoples are being displaced from their original territories for political or social reasons, so that metropolitan areas now contain larger indigenous populations than do Native American reservations. There are significant implications for indigenous identity in this population shift. I believe it is not only possible, but in our best interests, to seek to integrate the best of our traditional values with the best contemporary values.

Lurline Wailana McGregor

We are reclaiming our heritage—our spirituality, our language, our dances, our chants, our values, our knowledge of the ocean, and our traditional way of doing things. Even our history, which has always been told from the colonizer's perspective, is finally being told from our point of view. These are the things that are most important to us as Native Hawaiians. Thirty years ago, they were all but lost. Today they are flourishing. I work in television, which on one hand is nothing more than a modern way to tell stories, but in the larger realm is the modern-day colonizer. In the past, Hawaiians were put in front of the camera as background characters—never the heroes— adding to negative stereotypes. Today we are increasingly behind the camera, telling stories from our points of view; we are the main characters. There is a lot of reason to be hopeful in the midst of our social and economic problems. The stronger we become in our culture, the healthier we will become as a people and the more sovereign we can become in our thinking. There is still a long road ahead, but we have been here much longer than our Western colonizers, and there is no reason to believe we can't prevail.

the way home

Jaune Quick-to-See Smith

The other day I saw an Asian Indian woman on television who does nothing but hug people all day, every day, and people flock to her just for a hug. Many of our elders, such as Agnes Oshanee Kenmille, perform a similar function for all of us by reaching out daily to our tribe through their teaching, cultural sharing, advice, and caring attendance at all ceremonies and events. No event or ceremony is complete without at least one of our elders, if not several, in attendance. My tribe has given Oshanee a house free of any cost near the tribal headquarters and the college where she teaches. She has no college degree, probably not a high school diploma, but what she so generously shares is priceless and cannot be found in books anyway.

In our Native communities, the richest person is the one who gives the most of themselves and of their financial resources. This important cultural signifier called "giving back" can't be put into operation unless the giver has plenty of reserve, financially and within themselves. This is a highly esteemed life that the outside community doesn't understand. Sayings such as "saving for a rainy day" or "getting ahead" aren't part of the traditional Native consciousness.

My cousin/brother Gerry Slater was a visionary and a "giving back" person who began adding cultural courses to the Salish Kootenai College curriculum until he was able to make every course express a relationship to Salish and Kootenai culture. Whether the course was science, math, forestry, nursing, language, beading, or hide tanning and tipi raising, it had a relationship to Salish and Kootenai culture. Early on Gerry realized that going to college was not in our cultural consciousness, and he set about creating a curriculum with time slots amenable to tribal daily life. First the women came, then he added much-needed courses on family life, which brought healing between men and women. In the 1970s, the Indian bars owned by whites running the length of my reservation would be full on a weeknight. But now, after twenty-five years of creative cultural education at the tribal college, there are mostly empty bars weeknights.

We were always a trading tribe, but today through Salish Kootenai

every day is a good day

College, we trade education, information, and technology with other tribes. There is a cultural revolution going on in Indian Country, and a great deal of innovation. There is an emphasis on the collective versus the individual and on the extended family instead of the nuclear family. It reminds me of what the great Shawnee chief Blue Jacket said, "A single twig breaks, but the bundle of twigs is strong."

Rosalie Little Thunder

The most important challenge we face this century is assuring our basic cultural survival within a society that has either denied or actively oppressed the perpetuation of our culture. After nearly two centuries of existence in an oppressive society, many indigenous peoples' sense of survival is constrained within the framework of American values, which promote a lifestyle of physical comfort and convenience at the expense of other human beings and the natural world. It is this long-term oppression that sometimes blinds us to the greater challenge of being responsible for the survival of humanity and all of the relatives. Because we are silenced and devalued, it is much harder to maintain our knowledge system and culture and pass it on to future generations.

The Lakota have a prayer emphasis, Mitakuye Oyas'in, which refers to the interrelationship of all beings. It is difficult to explain this concept to a people who have a tendency to want everything validated and explained by science. It is even harder to explain to English speakers that Mitakuye Oyas'in also encompasses the energy fields that hum with timelessness and the connectedness of déjà vu and premonition, of aya and ayaptan, and the multitude of unseen, unexplainable things that are carelessly tossed into the superstition heap by observers who do not understand.

In our beliefs, when a person does something hurtful, that act is marked, and in another time, another way it returns to visit the offender. Likewise, when one is compassionate and generous, that act also returns, perhaps not to that person (and it should not be expected to) but to others within that person's family or even to descendants. To do things without

the way home

ishikiei shui, or any expectation of reciprocity, is one of the hardest disciplines to achieve but one with the greatest rewards.

We trust that aya *is what happens and the behavior that "sets in" when there is trauma, as in the loss of a loved one to the Spirit World. It is said that one must be on the very best behavior for four days after the loved one departs, and this behavior will* aya *thereafter.* Ayaptan *is when a person talks of something that hasn't happened yet and they are inviting fate. I remember a young man playing with a pair of crutches, hobbling along with them, and a grandma saying, "Shee! Hecun shni ye, aniyaptnin ket kshto!" (Don't do that, you will cause it to happen to you.) Some time later, the young man sprained his ankle playing basketball.*

Nagi Ksapa is yet another complex skill, which means having a wise spirit and recalling, not just being ambushed, by ancestral memories and being able to sense future happenings. I remember my mother saying, "Atash nagi ksape shni, awacin shni cha" to indicate that a person was not focusing on acquiring this skill. Although this term was common in my Lakota world, adequate English to define it is elusive.

We used to be able to sense each other through body language, but among Lakota, it was more like telepathy. We were able to receive subtle messages and react according, even to slight movements, pauses in conversation, or silence. We knew that the insects in the ground surfaced after the thunder beings returned. Now we have radios and televisions on all day, and the telephone jangling. Our children panic in silence. Our challenge is to teach them to waableza, *to hear the silence and know when a smiling face hides a broken heart.*

And so, all things, all beings are interrelated, not only among human beings. For indigenous peoples, that sense of responsibility is for our relatives, the keystone species that shape and guide our lives. We heed the lessons of the ants and the trees and the wind and the Moon.

Things used to be in balance, but I am not sure we will ever be able to reach balance again, not in this society, in this time. The values are so far apart that "balance" would be an illusion. But still we must pass on our beliefs and our teachings to the next generation, even though this knowledge is at odds with the American dream. Balance is when we all have an account in good standing with spiritual commerce, and our ears, eyes, hearts, and spirits are in good working order. The challenge of passing on this knowledge is further compounded by years of oppression, dependence, and shame. But still, we are closer in time to a better way of life that we can still remember.

We should teach our young people that indigenous wisdom is valuable and will become even more so as time goes on. They should acquaint themselves with their own cultures and learn the language of their ancestors. The language holds many secrets that escape English translation. The spirituality of their own people will help them see through the illusions of "success" as defined by Euro-Americans.

Our greatest challenge is to preserve that wisdom for a time when such wisdom will be desperately needed again. We are now in a time when humanity's ego has risen to dangerous levels of self-destruction. We are destroying that which sustains us, killing off different species and inflicting more and more painful wounds on the Earth. Many indigenous peoples' prophecies speak of the cleansing of the Earth. It probably won't happen in my lifetime, but I pass on the silent cheer, "Yes." Though for my children and grandchildren, I still whisper a silent prayer that maybe, just maybe, we as indigenous people can hold on to our beliefs and perhaps survive to become good relatives of all living things. Expecting to be heard by the American masses is perhaps unrealistic. Our values are too threatening to the American sense of comfort and sense of self.

I've given years of thought and research to defining the Lakota (and perhaps the indigenous) universe, and if the most important elements of that worldview are passed on to a few of the next generation, I would be one happy spirit. I deeply feel that the indigenous peoples of this planet are keepers of the cultural and spiritual map to another good place. If we all collectively contribute our energy, we will survive. I don't know if Euro-Americans will ever be able to listen and accept stories other than their own and accept that their way of life is not always right.

LaDonna Harris

We need to retribalize America because our cities are not working any more. There is no sense of belonging or of community. That is why people like McVeigh run off with these fringe groups and why gangs form, because it gives people a sense of belonging. After September 11, America was a community again for a brief period of time—though I was concerned about all the flags and people saying that God was only on the side of Americans. But America has no center. What's going to hold them together? No telling what will happen when they put Governor Tommy Thompson and the right-wing fundamentalist John Ashcroft together. And if you speak out against some of the things they are doing, you are branded as unpatriotic. One single congresswoman voted against giving Bush war powers to attack Afghanistan. She is now under armed guard.

Ella Mulford

To restore balance in our communities, I believe that our philosophies, practices, and protocols that have been around since life began must survive. Our traditional stories include many lessons that were learned by our ancestors. By respecting our stories, we may be able to avoid similar hardships that come with the lessons. I believe our generation today does not consider indigenous knowledge as significant, important, worthy, and of value to our present way of life. Many of us are forgetting some very simple principles that are important to our survival. We are losing our belief in our way of life. Some of the things we are forgetting are that we are a part of something bigger, and that we are a continuation of our ancestors. Not only are we connected in the physical to all things in the present, but we are also connected to our past and future. We need to bring our indigenous knowledge forward as a means for our survival. This does not mean we go back to living like we did in the past, it means we bring forward our ancestors' way of thought and actions. We must change our way of thought and actions if we are going to survive.

every day is a good day

Debra LaFountaine

We have to respect the natural laws of the universe and protect all living things and support those things in the natural world that support us. We are allowing the destruction of the very systems that we need to stay alive—water, air, trees, animals—as if they were of no consequence to us. There has to be a better understanding of the environment. We need to keep the culture and traditions alive and pay attention to the wisdom of the elders about how to live our lives. We have to respect the natural laws of the universe, share, and don't take more than we need, then everything will be restored, including our relationship with the Creator.

Chinook Blessing Litany

We call upon the Earth, our planet home, with its
beautiful depths and soaring heights, its vitality and
abundance of life, and together we ask that it
Teach us, and show us the Way

We call upon the mountains, the Cascades and the
Olympics, the high green valleys and meadows filled
with wildflowers, the snows that never melt, the
summits of intense silence, and we ask that they
Teach us, and show us the Way

We call upon the waters that rim the Earth, horizon to
horizon, that flow in our rivers and streams, that fall
upon our gardens and fields and
ask that they
Teach us, and show us the Way

We call upon the land which grows our food, the
nurturing soil, the fertile fields, the abundant gardens
and orchards, and ask that they
Teach us, and show us the Way

*We call upon the forests, the great trees reaching
strongly to the sky with Earth in their roots and the
heavens in their branches, the fir and the pine and the
cedar, and we ask them to*
Teach us, and show us the Way

---

*We call upon the creatures of the fields and the forests
and the seas, our brothers and sisters the wolves and
the deer, the eagle and dove, the great whales and the
dolphin, the beautiful orca and salmon who share our
Northwest home, and ask them to*
Teach us, and show us the Way

---

*We call upon those who have lived on this Earth, our
ancestors and our friends, who dreamed the best for
future generations, and upon whose lives our lives are
built, and with thanksgiving, we call upon them to*
Teach us, and show us the Way

---

*And lastly, we call upon all that we hold most sacred,
the presence and power of the Great Spirit of love and
truth, which flows through all the universe ... to be
with us to*
Teach us, and show us the Way

the way home

Linda Aranaydo, Muscogee Creek (physician)

Mary and Carrie Dann, Western Shoshone (traditionalists)

Angela Gonzales, Hopi (professor)

Joy Harjo, Muscogee Creek/Cherokee (poet/musician)

LaDonna Harris, Comanche (warrior)

Sarah James, Nee'Tsaii Gwich'in (human rights activist)

Debra LaFountaine, Ojibway (environmentalist)

Rosalie Little Thunder, Lakota (Lakota linguist/artist)

Lurline Wailana McGregor, Native Hawaiian (television producer)

Beatrice Medicine, Lakota (anthropologist)

Ella Mulford, Navajo (biologist)

Jaune Quick-to-See Smith, Salish Flathead (artist)

Audrey Shenandoah, Onondaga (Clan Mother)

Joanne Shenandoah, Oneida (musician)

Gail Small (Head Chief Woman), Northern Cheyenne (environmental activist)

Faith Smith, Ojibway (educator)

Florence Soap, Cherokee (grandmother)

Octaviana Valenzuela Trujillo, Pascua Yaqui (educator)

every day is a good day

women at the gathering

Biographies

It was a privilege and an honor to photograph most of the women in this book and listen to their conversations with Wilma about life, love, and spirituality. Every single woman in the book is unique and special, and they do represent the idea that no matter what happens, we should consider every day a good day. When I am faced with a challenge, I often draw on the lessons I learned from the women included in this book.

When we visited Bea Medicine at the home of her sister, Grace, they were preparing for an upcoming giveaway. The apartment was filled with dozens of carefully selected items to give to people they honor and care about. And when Wilma came back from the home of Mary and Carrie Dann, she spoke about the wonderful experience of speaking with the Dann sisters over a delicious jackrabbit lunch while their grandchildren laughed, played, and hopped on and off their laps. And I recall walking along the beach in Hawaii searching for a perfect spot to photograph Lurline McGregor. She wanted to be photographed with the water and black rocks in the background because the land, natural world, and water are an important part of her identity.

It gives me great pleasure to know the conversations of these women will be of assistance to people who struggle each day to try to find some peace of mind in a very complex world. It is my sincere hope that the people who see the photos and read the book will find many things of value that can be incorporated into their own lives. We need this book.

—Charlie Soap

Love is a part of everyone's humanity. A newborn baby has a basic need to be loved and to love back. I would like to be able to express that part of me in everything I do. ... So, as a physician, when I am exploring the nature of healing I have to begin with myself.

Linda Aranaydo

Linda Aranaydo is Muscogee Creek, Kialegee Tribal Town, Bear Clan. She is a physician, a patient-centered healer who conducts her practice within the context of her Muscogee Creek values. She practices medicine with the same sense of ethics, warmth, love, and justice that led her to join the Poor People's March in 1968 and the occupation of Alcatraz Island in 1969. Though she has served as medical director of several important health organizations, she prefers family practice.

For more than a decade Dr. Aranaydo served as teacher and then center supervisor at the Hintil KuuCa Children's Center for Native American Children (Native American Parent Preschool) in Oakland, California.

Dr. Aranaydo received her bachelor's degree and elementary teaching credentials from the University of California at Berkeley, a second bachelor's degree in biology from Mills College, and an M.D. from the University of California San Francisco School of Medicine.

biographies

Western Shoshone women are taught that a woman is like the Earth: she gives and nurtures life. The Earth and women have the same properties. The Earth provides for us, just as we provide for our children. The way we were taught, if the Earth is treated with disrespect by a woman, she is disrespecting herself. We are one and the same.

every day is a good day

Mary and Carrie Dann

Mary and Carrie Dann are Western Shoshone ranchers who have led a forty-year battle to retain their ancestral homelands, using whatever peaceful means were available to them, including demonstrations and the courts. The battle began in 1973 when the United States Bureau of Land Management came out to their ranch on Western Shoshone land and asked them to obtain grazing permits and pay grazing fees for their cattle. They argued that the cattle were grazing on Western Shoshone land. The Bureau of Land Management sued them for trespassing and the battle was engaged.

Fluent in the Western Shoshone language, the Dann sisters have lived their lives and conducted their work according to traditional Western Shoshone lifeways. Their story has appeared in dozens of publications and in several documentaries, including one narrated by Robert Redford. In 1993 they received the Right Livelihood Award, which is often called the alternative Nobel Prize.

biographies

I am really opposed to this idea of being either a.) Indian or

b.) non-Indian. I think that it can always be a blending of

the two cultures. You take what is good from both cultures and

it makes you a better person.

every day is a good day

Dr. Angela Gonzales

Dr. Angela Gonzales is a member of the Hopi Nation. She is an assistant professor at Cornell University and former chair of the Department of American Indian Studies at San Francisco State University. She has presented a number of papers on American Indian identity issues at important conferences. Her dissertation examines the intricate issues of individual and collective American Indian self-definition and membership boundaries.

Dr. Gonzales has also taught courses on issues of American Indian ethnicity and identity, religion, and philosophy. She has worked for the Hopi Tribe in education, research, and planning.

Dr. Gonzales has an undergraduate degree in sociology, double master's degrees from Harvard University in sociology and education, and a Ph.D. in sociology from Harvard University.

biographies

I believe love is the strongest force in the world. It is the

word and the concept I substitute for God. In the Muscogee

language, vnokeckv translates as "an overriding compassion"

and is the root of Muscogee philosophy.

every day is a good day

Joy Harjo

Joy Harjo is an enrolled member of the Muscogee Creek Nation. She is related to the Tiger Clan through her father. Her Cherokee mother does not recall her clan. She is one of the most prominent Native writers of our time. She has won a number of literary awards and has published several books of poetry, including her most recent, *How We Became Human, New and Selected Poems*. She has also written children's books and published an anthology of Native Women's writing, *Reinventing the Enemy's Language*. She is currently working on a book of short stories.

Ms. Harjo is an accomplished musician whose first band, Poetic Justice, produced the CD *Letter from the End of the Twentieth Century*. She continues to perform professionally with her present band, Joy Harjo and Her Band.

Ms. Harjo has an undergraduate degree in creative writing and an MFA from the University of Iowa Writers' Workshop. She credits her attendance at the Institute of American Indian Arts in Santa Fe, which was then a high school, with saving her from a life of addiction and suicide.

biographies

I never think about losing anybody, even an adversary. I may never have them as a close friend, but I don't lose them. People in my life are valuable. In the Comanche way, if you have hurt someone, you will also be hurt until you go back and try to reinstate that relationship or make it right in some way.

LaDonna Harris

LaDonna Harris is an enrolled member of the Comanche Nation and is a remarkable stateswoman and national leader who has enriched the lives of thousands by building Native American, civil rights, environmental, women's rights, and peace movement coalitions that create change. She is a consistent and ardent advocate on behalf of indigenous people.

Ms. Harris began her public service as the wife of U.S. Senator Fred Harris. Her partnership with Senator Harris made her a strong force in Congress, where she was instrumental in the return of the Taos Blue Lake to the people of Taos Pueblo and to the Menominee Tribe in regaining their federal recognition. Her guiding influence on both pieces of legislation led to landmark laws that set a precedent that continues to guide Indian policy. She was also instrumental in the adoption of official Indian policies by the Environmental Protection Agency, the Department of Energy, and the Department of Agriculture.

She has served on dozens of national and international boards and founded or cofounded dozens of organizations including the Americans for Indian Opportunity, the National Women's Political Caucus, and a highly successful Native American leadership program.

biographies

The main difference between us and people in the larger society

is that indigenous people have a home, a homeland we share with

people we are related to. ...The Creator put us where we are to

take care of this part of the world.

every day is a good day

Sarah James

Sarah James is Nee'Tsaii Gwich'in. In 1988 she was selected by tribal leaders and elders to be an advocate for and defender of the Arctic Coastal Plains and the birthplace of the porcupine caribou. In that capacity she has testified before Congress, appeared in documentaries, on national news programs, and in the print media. She has presented countless lectures on the critical need to protect the area that has come to be known as the Arctic National Wildlife Refuge.

She serves on a number of boards, including the Gwich'in Steering Committee, the Environmental Justice Advisory Board, the Council of Athabascan Tribal Governments, the Native Village of Venetie Tribal Government, and many other boards and committees related to her battle to protect her homelands. A speaker of Gwich'in, she has also worked with youth to promote the use of indigenous languages and to teach traditional Gwich'in lifeways. She has been awarded the Charles Bannerman Memorial Fellowship, Ford Foundation's Leadership for a Changing World Fellowship, and she has won the Goldman Environmental Award.

biographies

As I became more focused on the message of the elders, I learned that peace starts from within and works its way out. If one begins to heal oneself, to walk one's own path and understand one's purpose, the rest will follow.

every day is a good day

Debra LaFountaine

Debra LaFountaine is a member of the Turtle Mountain Chippewa Tribe. She spent twelve years in the physical development of communities as a city planner and civil engineering technician and eight years in the social and organizational development of communities through the implementation of wellness programs designed to promote the mental, emotional, physical, and spiritual health of individuals and communities based on teachings of Native American elders.

She has helped to design and implement community development strategies based on Native American concepts and principles that promoted community pride and commitment to a common vision. She has also developed a range of workshops and conferences dealing with physical and social development of communities, leadership, cultural values, unity, substance abuse, and healing.

Ms. LaFountaine has a degree in urban and regional planning from Eastern Washington University.

biographies

I've given years of thought and research to defining the Lakota (and perhaps the indigenous) universe, and if the most important elements of that worldview are passed on to a few of the next generation, I would be one happy spirit. I deeply feel that the indigenous peoples of this planet are keepers of the cultural and spiritual map to another good place. If we all collectively contribute our energy, we will survive.

every day is a good day

Rosalie Little Thunder

Rosalie Little Thunder, Sicangu Lakota, is a very prominent bead artist whose designs are derived from her extensive research on early pre-reservation beadwork. Her award-winning art has been featured in the Royal Museum of Scotland, Carnegie Museum, the Heard Museum, the Santa Fe Indian Market, and many other prestigious institutions. She is an educator who not only teaches Lakota, she trains others to teach the language. She is also a grassroots community activist who has devoted much of her adult life to advocacy for the survival of buffalo. She has led the struggle to save the last free bison herd in Yellowstone Park, Montana. In 1999, she led a 507-mile march across Montana in honor of the 1,100 Yellowstone buffalo slaughtered that year by the Montana Department of Livestock. In the fall of 2004, she will lead another walk to thank all those who have supported the buffalo and who supported the first walk. Recently Rosalie advised and encouraged the United Nations Permanent Forum on Indigenous Issues to participate in a Global Campaign to Protect the Sacred Species of Indigenous Peoples. Rosalie serves as chair of the Board of Directors of the Seventh Generation Fund. She has won many awards for her art and for her activism, including the Bannerman Award.

biographies

Traditional indigenous knowledge systems and stories acknowledge that

the rivers, rocks, trees, plant life, and celestial world are alive with spirit

and meaning. When traditional indigenous people speak of their relatives,

they are referring to every living thing, not just human kinship. The very

identity of traditional tribal people is derived from the natural world,

the land, and the community. They understand their own insignificance

in the totality of things.

every day is a good day

Wilma Mankiller

Wilma Mankiller, Cherokee, was an author, activist, and served for ten years as the principal chief of the Cherokee Nation. Her roots were planted deeply in the rural community of Mankiller Flats in Adair County, Oklahoma, where she spent most of her life. She was honored with many awards, including the Presidential Medal of Freedom, and received eighteen honorary doctorates from such esteemed institutions as Yale University, Dartmouth College, and Smith College.

Ms. Mankiller coauthored *Mankiller: A Chief and Her People* and coedited *A Reader's Companion to U.S. Women's History*, as well as publishing more than a dozen articles in journals and newspapers. She was a trustee of the Ford Foundation and the Freedom Forum. Ms. Mankiller lived on the Mankiller family allotment with her husband, Charlie Soap. She passed away in 2010.

biographies

People must embrace the spiritual nature of love if they are to truly know and understand its power. Love can move mountains. It nourishes people's souls more profoundly than material acquisitions could ever hope to do.

every day is a good day

Lurline Wailana McGregor

Lurline Wailana McGregor, a Native Hawaiian, served as legislative director for a congressman from Hawai'i, and later became a professional staff member for U.S. Senator Daniel K. Inouye when he became chair of the Senate Select Committee on Indian Affairs. Her work as a professional staff member focused primarily on Native Hawaiian cultural issues. Ultimately her passion for those issues led her to produce videos and television programs on Native Hawaiian issues and culture. Her film, *Hokule'A—Guiding Star*, pays tribute to the historic and contemporary sailing skills of traditional Native Hawaiians by tracking the voyage of Hokule'a. Ms. McGregor is also a canoeist.

When she returned to Hawai'i in 1992, her combination of production and political experience led her to become the executive director of Pacific Islanders in Communications, a minority consortium whose mission is to increase the amount of programming by and about indigenous Pacific Islanders on National Public Television. She currently serves as president/CEO of 'Olelo Community Television, a community cable access station that serves the island of O'ahu.

Ms. McGregor's formal education includes attendance at some of the best schools in the country and the Sorbonne in Paris, France.

biographies

*To be a good Lakota woman and for our brothers to be good Lakota men,
we have to help each other. ... Men and women are leaders and I feel
very strongly that we must maintain respect and honor between males
and females and transmit that to our children.*

Dr. Beatrice Medicine

Dr. Beatrice Medicine, a member of the Standing Rock Sioux Tribe of North and South Dakota, has had a long and exemplary academic career. She has taught at more than thirty universities and colleges, where she has touched the lives of thousands of students. She has published more than ninety journal articles, contributed to more than twenty books, and traveled extensively throughout the world to present lectures on a range of Native American issues. She produced an award-winning film, *Plains Indians*, in Russia.

Dr. Medicine has served on a number of commissions that shaped public policy, including the Canadian Parliament's Royal Commission on Aboriginal Peoples, the largest indigenous study undertaken by a governmental body. She is renowned as a prominent indigenous anthropologist, author, and lecturer. However, one of her most significant honors is that she was asked by her tribal Native religious practitioners to serve as the Sacred Pipe Woman for the 1977 Sun Dance.

Dr. Medicine earned undergraduate degrees in education, art, and history at South Dakota State University, master's degrees in sociology and anthropology at Michigan State University, and a Ph.D. in cultural anthropology from the University of Wisconsin.

biographies

Not only are we connected in the physical to all things in the present, but we are also connected to our past and future. We need to bring our indigenous knowledge forward as a means for our survival. This does not mean we go back to living like we did in the past, it means we bring forward our ancestors' way of thought and actions. We must change our way of thought and actions if we are going to survive.

every day is a good day

Ella Mulford

Ella Mulford, a member of the Diné (Navajo) Nation, is a Ta'neeszahnii and born for Tt'aashci'i and related to To'tosohnii and Tl'izila'ni. She has twenty-four years of experience working in environmental protection. Her areas of specialty include tribal governments and community relations, environmental regulatory compliance, and pollution prevention. Her positive outlook on life comes from her people, especially her grandparents.

Recently Ms. Mulford worked directly with wise and knowledgeable indigenous elders on determining the best possible solutions to current environmental issues. Additionally, she connected indigenous elders with youth to start the process of learning for the youth.

Ms. Mulford works with the U.S. Environmental Protection Agency. She has a bachelor's degree in biology from Northern Arizona University.

biographies

The Sacred isn't housed in a building or worn around your neck or something in the sky. The Sacred is the here and now we reside in, all breathing the same air, all imbibing the same water and made of the same earth with "the life force" flowing through all living things.

every day is a good day

Jaune Quick-to-See Smith

Jaune Quick-to-See Smith is an enrolled Flathead Salish. She is an internationally celebrated painter/printmaker and lecturer on American Indian contemporary art. Her art is in public collections at the Museum of Mankind in Vienna, Austria; the Museum of Modern Art in New York; the National Museum of American Art in Washington, D.C.; as well as many other prestigious institutions throughout the world. Equally important, she has used her considerable creativity and intellectual skills to form two cooperatives, has organized a number of touring exhibits, and has served as curator for many others. She has presented lectures at more than 150 universities, museums, and conferences internationally.

She has received honorary doctorates from the Pennsylvania Academy of Art and the Minneapolis College of Art and Design among her many honors and awards. Her artwork has been reviewed by the *Village Voice* and the *New York Times* and has been featured in numerous documentaries and films.

Ms. Quick-to-See Smith received a bachelor's degree in art education and a master's degree in art from the University of New Mexico.

biographies

When we acknowledge all the rest of Creation, we are acknowledging

their existence as equals to us. We are not the strongest of everything

in life's cycle. Man thinks he is superior and dominant over everything,

even moving the Earth or trees at his discretion, and that everything else

in Creation is a commodity that he can use or make money on.

And that is why the world is out of balance.

every day is a good day

Audrey Shenandoah

Audrey Shenandoah, Onondaga, is first and foremost a Clan Mother with responsibility to members of her clan and her nation. Her duties include passing along the longhouse tradition, selecting leaders, and maintaining harmony in the clan. She is one of the most respected traditional indigenous leaders of our time. Audrey teaches the Onondaga language and traditional lifeways to people in her community, especially children. For many years she taught Onondaga language and culture at the Onondaga School near Nedrow.

Besides her duties as a Clan Mother, she has also traveled extensively to present messages on the Haudenosaunee worldview, including a presentation in Moscow in 1992 as a prelude to the 1992 Earth Summit in Rio de Janeiro. She is an internationally recognized lecturer on environmental issues and for peaceful resolution of world conflicts. She and her daughter, Jeanne, have been featured in many news articles and numerous film documentaries.

biographies

There is nothing more beautiful in life than experiencing ceremonies with my loved ones. No matter what is going on in our lives, we remain strong because we come from such a powerfully sound place. When we step inside the longhouse, we leave outside the door any angry feelings or other things we disagree on and come together with a good mind to celebrate this beautiful gift of life together.

every day is a good day

Joanne Shenandoah

Joanne Shenandoah, a member of the Oneida Nation, is a highly accomplished composer, author, and musician. She was named artist of the year at the Nammy's and her CD, *Peacemakers Journey*, was nominated for an Emmy. Among significant appearances around the world, she opened the 1994 Woodstock conference and performed at the 1993 and 1997 presidential inaugural events. She has been featured in a number of television productions. She has a long list of awards and honors, including an honorary doctorate from Syracuse University.

Joanne is an articulate spokesperson for peace and compassion. She is a relatively soft-spoken warrior and ardent advocate for her people. She has carried on a long family tradition of support for preserving traditional lifeways and the traditional land base of the Oneida people.

biographies

There is a profound spiritual dimension to our natural environment, and
without it, the war would not be worth fighting. ... We look forward to
the seasons and know what is coming into harvest or blooming, and we
know and appreciate the beauty of the land.

every day is a good day

Gail Small (Head Chief Woman)

Gail Small is a member of the Northern Cheyenne Nation. She is an attorney and tireless worker for environmental justice who directs Native Action, one of the oldest and most successful reservation-based nonprofit organizations in Indian Country. For literally her entire adult life she has waged an ongoing legal and political battle to protect her homelands from large extractive and often exploitive energy companies.

Ms. Small served on the Federal Reserve Board of Governors, Consumer Advisory Council; on the Environmental Justice Committee of the Environmental Protection Agency; and as a councilwoman on the Northern Cheyenne Tribal Council. Ms. Small and Native Action were instrumental in securing a high school on the reservation, conducting a nationally recognized voter registration and education project, and organizing a Rock the Vote concert, and together have undertaken a number of leadership programs for children and youth.

Ms. Small received her bachelor's degree from the University of Montana and her Juris Doctor from the University of Oregon School of Law.

biographies

Women build more bridges and try to find connections instead of confrontation. Women have to negotiate all the time, from the moment we get up until we go to bed at night. We may not like everybody, but we can build a long-term agenda without camps or factions.

every day is a good day

Faith Smith

Faith Smith, Ojibway, and is president and founder of NAES College (Native American Educational Services College), a private, Indian-controlled bachelor degree–granting institution based in Chicago, Illinois. NAES College has developed satellite campuses in Minneapolis, Minnesota; Popular, Montana; and Keshena, Wisconsin.

In addition to her groundbreaking development of NAES College, Ms. Smith has served as a consultant to the Kellogg Foundation, the Northwest Area Foundation, and a number of other national organizations. She has won a number of significant awards for community service, including the Peace through Justice Award/Clergy and Laity Concerned, the Distinguished Alumni Award from Purdue University, and the Community Service Fellowship Award from the Chicago Community Trust.

Ms. Smith received her bachelor's degree in education from Purdue University and a master's degree in social science from the University of Chicago.

biographies

I consider myself a prayerful person. When I pray, I always pray to love

all people. Some people claim that they love, but it is not from their

heart. By carefully observing a person, one can tell if they have love

within them. I pray that people will learn to love one another.

every day is a good day

Florence Soap

Florence Soap was a Cherokee elder, healer, gospel singer, mother, and grandmother. She was one of the few remaining Cherokee people who could not only speak fluent Cherokee, but also could read and write it. Ms. Soap was raised in a time when both girls and boys hunted and gathered most of their food, were treated by Cherokee healers for their physical and mental illnesses, and relied on family, neighbors, and friends for survival. As a girl she learned to hunt, do farm work, manage horses, quilt, and can vegetables, fruits, and jellies—a practice she continued well into her eighties.

Ms. Soap organized a cooperative organization that raised and managed funds to pay for medical expenses and medicines of its members. As a member of the Cherokee Choir, she helped raise thousands of dollars for Cherokee families in crisis and traveled to the Smithsonian Museum in Washington, D.C., to perform.

biographies

My personal identity as a woman and a human is very tied to my people. I hope to be remembered as a Yaqui (Yoeme) from the community of Guadalupe who was truly bicultural, bicognitive, and bilingual. If my people speak of me in the distant future, I hope they will say I was a reasonable person and that I was not afraid to challenge injustice.

Octaviana Valenzuela Trujillo

Octaviana Valenzuela Trujillo is Pascua Yaqui from the Guadalupe Community of Arizona. In 1992, Octaviana was elected as the first woman vice chair.

For more than three decades she has worked to develop educational programs for minority and multicultural populations, particularly Native Americans. She received a Ph.D. in curriculum and instruction from Arizona State University. She is currently professor and chair of the Applied Indigenous Studies Department at Northern Arizona University. Her primary academic focus is the role of multilingual, multicultural language and literacy development in minority and indigenous community development efforts.

Her studies have been augmented during summers through such activities as a Fulbright Fellowship in India, attending the Instituto Cultural de Guanajuato in Mexico, participating in study sessions of the International Institute of Human Rights in Strasbourg, France, and the Salzburg Institute in Austria, as well as serving as a delegate of the UN Beijing Forum on Women. She has traveled extensively for her own research interests, as a Kellogg Leadership Fellow, and in conjunction with human rights delegations in Chiapas, Mexico, and Cauca, Colombia.

biographies

bibliography

Akwesasne Notes, ed. *Basic Call to Consciousness*. Summertown, TN: Book
   Publishing Company, 1978.

Brant, Beth. *A Gathering of Spirit*. Ann Arbor, MI: Firebrand Books, 1988.

Deloria Jr., Vine. *For This Land*. New York: Routledge, 1999.

George-Kanentiio, Doug. *Iroquois Culture and Commentary*. Santa Fe, NM:
   Clear Light Publishers, 2000.

Goldsmith, Edward. *The Way: An Ecological World-View*. Athens, GA: University
   of Georgia Press, 1992.

LaDuke, Winona. *All Our Relations*. Cambridge, MA: South End Press, 1999.

Medicine, Beatrice. *Learning to Be an Anthropologist and Remaining Native*.
   Champaign, IL: University of Illinois Press, 2001.

Mohawk, John C. *Utopian Legacies: A History of Conquest and Oppression in the
   Western World*. Santa Fe, NM: Clear Light Publishers, 2000.

Roesch Wagner, Sally. *The Untold Story of the Iroquois Influence on Early
   Feminists*. Aberdeen, SD: Sky Carrier Press, 1996.

Strickland, Rennard. *Fire and Spirits*. Norman, OK: University of Oklahoma
   Press, 1975.

Viola, Herman J. *Diplomats in Buckskin.* Washington, D.C.: Smithsonian Institute Press, 1981.

Wallace, Paul. *White Roots of Peace: The Iroquois Book of Life.* Santa Fe, NM: Clear Light Publishers, 1996.

Weatherford, Jack. *Indian Givers.* New York: Ballantine Books, 1988.

Weiss, Stefanie Iris. *The Beauty Myth.* New York: The Rosen Publishing Group, 2000.